ONE PHYSICIAN'S JOURNEY FROM BURNOUT TO BLISS
REVEALS THE CREATIVE MUSE IN ALL OF US

RIGHT BRAIN
RESCUE

LARA SALYER, DO, IFMCP

Date Published: September 27, 2020

Cover Design by 100Covers.com
Interior Design by FormattedBooks.com

ISBN: *978-1-7354498-0-7*

CONTENTS

PROLOGUE

I was entombed in my body. My thoughts floating in the murky recesses of my tired brain. My limbs, heavy and awkward. Everywhere my eyes looked, it was through a foggy lens of shame. The air was oppressive. Each inhale felt downtrodden. Each exhale, a defeat.

"Hey, Mom, guess what?!" my child chirped from between overstuffed bags of groceries in the back seat.

I strained my eyes to peek in the rearview mirror. That effort was so enormous, they quickly fell back onto the horizon.

"What, sweetie?" My false perky voice betrayed me. While his hands clutched a lemonade, my hands clutched the steering wheel. The road before me felt exasperatingly long and tortuous. When did it become so difficult to operate a motor vehicle?

The sun was setting without my permission, *again*. Soon, I would collapse into unconsciousness, and then be forced awake by my alarm to begin another Monday. No one should feel this way. It's supposed to get better. I had worked *so hard* to get here.

"Mom! Did you hear what I said?" His voice was insistent.

I shook my head silently as I pulled into our driveway, blinking back tears. I had wanted to be a doctor since the fifth grade. I toiled away for decades. *Decades.* I yearned for this so badly, I hadn't even considered marriage or children until the universe sent me a man that changed my mind. He was hooked on the same trajectory and understood the sacrifices.

It had been fifteen years since I graduated medical school. I should have had it all figured out by now. I jumped through every hoop and attended every resiliency training. This should be the land of milk and honey, but instead it's cows and bees. I still have to work for that milk and honey.

I'm uncomfortably miserable.

"If your mouth is full of lemonade, it's impossible to smile!" my child proclaimed, lemonade dripping from his chin.

That's it.

I'm too full.

And it has become impossible to smile.

How did I get here?

Let's retrace my steps....

CHAPTER ONE
FORESHADOWING

I was about to perform reconstructive surgery, to change someone's life forever. My hands were poised above the body, and my knees felt wobbly. I inhaled briskly, and the scent of the sharp, sterile air shocked my lungs. Suddenly, I was acutely aware of all my senses: the scratchy fabric of the standard-issued uniform against my back, the thud of my heart against my rib cage, the leftover taste of a ham-and-swiss sandwich in my mouth. Music softly played in the background, the song "We are the World."

It was 1984, and I was about to complete the world's first nose transplant. I was only nine years old.

"Hold still," I muttered to my own pair of trembling hands. I reached forward, extending a gloved fingertip to adjust the contour of the patient's nose. I gently straightened its bridge. "There. Much better," I commented to the staff in the operating room. Crowds had gathered to witness my unusual surgical techniques. I stepped back and tilted my head to the side for better perspective.

"Almost, but not quite," I uttered. I smoothed the left nostril edge to match the right. "There. Perfection!" I proudly gazed at the majestic nose I created, as if stolen from a Grecian statue.

Triumphant, I backed away from the operating table. There was a collective exhale in the room and then a flash of newspaper cameras and thundering applause.

Without warning, the patient wiggled right off the operating room table and the fictitious crowd vanished. The fresh Silly Putty "nose" slid off my little brother's face and bounced to the ground. He darted down the hallway as the only surgical assistant—my sister—shrugged.

With the fantasy completely over, I chased after him, but Grandpa's hallways were labyrinthine. His home was an enormous collection of mystery, each room guarded with a heavy door and intricate doorknob. My hands twisted each one desperately as I peeked into vacant rooms, searching for my escaped "patient." Opening door after door, revealing rooms like backdrops to different movie genres: sticky pleather couches paired with a faded avocado green rug (seventies drama). A utilitarian desk topped with mountains of invoices and a huddle of half-empty coffee mugs (mystery/suspense). A kitchen with flour scattered on the floor and broken eggs (comedy).

Finally, the last room. The horror genre. I opened the door slowly.

Rows of shiny caskets were arranged as neatly as a parking lot. Suddenly, my brother emerged from behind a funeral wreath, giggling as he skirted past.

My childhood wasn't quite like others. While my grade school friends' Barbies drove shiny red Corvettes and lived in extravagant dream houses, mine slept in mini-coffins and had pretend funerals. In middle school, my friends had grandparents who baked cookies and smelled of vanilla and cinnamon when they gave hugs. An aroma of formaldehyde and methanol wafted from my grandparents with each polite nod.

If you have one hour left to live, spend it in a funeral home. It would last forever.

As a kid, most of us could fill that hour easily. We were born masters of play and quickly filled in the blanks with our imagination. We loved *Mad Libs, Choose Your Own Adventure* books, and the two words "free" and "time"—the "negative space" that remains an essential element to any creative endeavor.

Sometime after we hear, "The floor is lava," but before "Can I see your ID," we change. Adults wouldn't know what to do with the gift of an hour (probably spend it "unsubscribing" from email lists). Adults don't do well with fill-in-the-blanks or empty canvases. It makes us uncomfortable, so we fill the space. We clap during the silence between orchestral pieces. We oversaturate our photos with filters. We impatiently ask, "So when are you getting married?" as soon as our friends are dating (and then follow with "When are you having a baby?" after they throw the garter belt).

Growing older, we don't feel the shrinking of our imagination at first. It's silent and impalpable, replaced by the well-rehearsed confidence of maturity. Adulthood is marked by knowing. Deciding. Analyzing. Leaving space for wonder and curiosity is simply too risky and unknown. Having negative space is acknowledging there is no answer, but many possibilities. It's admitting you have a choice in what note to play next, which word to write or color to paint.

Negative space is where the magic happens, and adults rush through it. What finish line are we rushing toward? Death? In my childhood, death was an invisible force that could fill those negative spaces without warning. Grandpa's house of movie genres would be transformed overnight into a gathering where everyone stared at a big, open box containing a sentimental gift inside. Death was kinda like a bizarrely goth alternative Santa Claus that reminded everyone to make use of those wondrous spaces while you had them.

CHAPTER TWO

GROWING UP WITH DEATH

Decay is our measuring stick. Doctors, morticians, and artists all calculate their impact by comparing against this expiration date. When your body slumps before a doctor—a sickly heap of fever, cough, and phlegm—you are essentially asking, "Really, how *close to Death* am I?!" Similarly, as your cold body is on display before a mortician, your question is, "How *close to Life* can you make me look?"

This job belonged to my mother.

As a young girl, I'd stand on my tiptoes, craning my neck to watch her sweep cerulean eye shadow across lids and smear foundation on sunken cheeks. While my high school friends resorted to secondhand eye shadow instruction from the pages of *Teen* magazine, I learned by watching my mom transform the face of a corpse with her skilled makeup application. My mother's gentle and methodical lipstick application entranced me. Back and forth. Slowly outlining the cupid's bow of a mouth. Delicately tracing the arch in a feathery eyebrow. Until, wondrously, the corpse's vacant mask appeared serenely lifelike.

With her artistry complete, no one could spot the thin line of super glue keeping the embalmed lips from springing open, or the plastic eye caps that gave the appearance of eyeballs peacefully resting in sockets.

As I grew older, I pondered their last moments before this transition. What was the final word they spoke? Who received their last hug? What were they thinking when they realized their mortal roller-coaster ride was coming to a full and complete stop?

Appearances are everything. Even in death. Stand around any funeral home and you'll hear comments like:

"That spring palette is the wrong tone for Edna's winter skin."
"Did they use hypoallergenic cosmetics for Gladys?"
"Fred's eyebrows never looked so magnificent."

As the grieving patrons milled around, I'd position myself behind the stairwell and peer between the railings, searching for the Mystery Guest. There was always one. They'd stand away from the crowd to avoid the family greeting line. You'd never see their signature in the guest book. Instead, they'd always keep a respectful distance. It was *these people* that spurred my imagination. I'd analyze their body language and expressions to compose a tortuous story.

One Mystery Lady arrived wearing a conservative pencil skirt and wool blazer. Her brunette hair, aged with silvery streaks, was pulled into an elegant bun. She removed her sunglasses and stepped to the casket, heels silent on the carpeted floor. Her eyes flanked by gentle wrinkles, she stared at the corpse's strong, masculine hands.

Maybe they worked together in a deli shop one summer in college. The first time she shook his warm hand, she was hooked. His touch was medicinal and melty. Watching him carve a turkey became a daily religious experience, but it was his earnest eyes that kept her at that wretchedly boring job.

Mystery Lady leaned closer, and a delicate tear dripped down her powdered cheek.

Perhaps instead, he was her enthusiastic grade-school piano teacher. As a foster child, she often felt isolated and alone. He inspired her to express her pent-up emotions through the ivory keys. He gave the most encompassing hugs. His arms felt like they encircled her twice over. Eventually, she went off to college and signed on with Tokyo Symphonic Orchestra decades later. She never did get a chance to thank him.

Mystery Lady paused, inhaled deeply, and dabbed her nose with a butter-yellow lace handkerchief.

Conceivably, he was her neighbor. They'd spend afternoons climbing oak trees and evenings catching fireflies. They'd cut tags off of stuffed animals to turn them "real" and talk to ghosts stuck in the abandoned house down the street. Hard to believe he only lived next door for a few months. His influence was what sparked her career in childhood psychology.

We fill our lives with "what ifs" and missed opportunities. A multitude of alternative lives, unexplored.

Mystery Lady buttoned up her secret and walked out the funeral parlor doors. Once all sadness had evaporated from the air, and the coffin was on its way below the dirt, Grandpa's funeral home would be a stoically empty space again.

Years later, at my mother's urging, I wandered the halls of my grandpa's home, on a mission for spare items to furnish my vacant college apartment. Tucked in a box, I discovered the Mystery Lady's forgotten butter-yellow lace handkerchief. I was tempted to keep it, but a recent viewing of *Amityville Horror* convinced me otherwise. I left the Mystery Lady's memories intact.

I continued my scavenger hunt and sniffed each upholstered ottoman and chair. After baking in years of formaldehyde air, nothing would pass the nostrils of my roommates without serious disdain. With the stale scent of perfumed chemicals in my nostrils, I only dared to accept a stainless steel whisk. It was the most neutral item I could find.

Stainless steel doesn't keep memories. It's easily cleansed of smell and fingerprints, and makes an unflappable witness in our human events. This explains why its cold surface gleams in hospitals and embalming rooms, and is evidence of how similar doctors and morticians can be as they deal with the full spectrum of death—from peaceful to senseless. Both professions serve communities and demand long hours, mounds of paperwork, and copious late-night phone calls.

Somewhere in either career, you'll inevitably find a person eating a bologna sandwich over a dead body.

And both start with the same question....

CHAPTER THREE

ALIVE OR DEAD?

"Is it alive or dead?"

I glanced around the room to recognize bewilderment in the eyes of my medical school classmates. At twenty-one years old, I had joined 125 other caffeinated bodies vibrating on their lab-stool perches, five per lab table.

The professor clarified, "Is *the table in front of you* alive…or dead?"

Twelve years of public school. Four years of college. To get *here*?!

To answer *this* question?

"Ignore the body bag resting on the table. We already understand the cadavers are deceased. I'm asking about the table. Is your table *alive*…or *dead*?" The professor removed a hand from his pocket and waved it in the air for extra dramatic flair.

His words expanded in the room like an awkward fart. We were embarrassed to smell it and too scared to comment on the obvious.

"Place your hand on the table surface in front of you. *Feel* it," he commanded.

One hundred and twenty-five pairs of hands synchronously reached forward. Hands attached to 125 distinctly unique brains, opinions, emotions, and energy; 125 different favorite ice cream flavors, political views, religious beliefs, and preferred music genres. And yet, it made no difference who the hands belonged to; we all had one thing in common. We had fallen for the same love: a career in modern medicine.

That afternoon, we had converged to finally meet our passionate infatuation. With wobbly knees and fluttery eyelashes, we were under the spell of a new relationship like lovestruck teens. This emotional moment was the result of decades of courting, but I didn't think it would start with heavy petting on a stainless steel table.

Like any good romantic drama, the foreplay started several hours earlier when we met the other participants vying for the attention of a medical career. We streamed into the large auditorium to pick a seat. I did what everyone would: locate a friendly face. No one wants to sit next to that grumpy outlier who would disagree with the four other doctor recommendations, right?

Unknowingly, I happened to pick the seat right in front of Future Husband.

The professor gave us a simple task: stand up and introduce yourself to the other students. A perfect antidote to our first-day jitters. We spent the next few hours learning about others in the room: pilots, researchers, world travelers, professors. We discovered who liked sashimi, who discovered the secret ingredient to a good microbrew lager, and who restored vintage cars by hand. Each person had a more unique story than the next.

I felt my mental block build. I didn't travel the Serengeti barefoot. I had never co-authored a medical research article on dysentery. What would be *my* opening line? Barbie funerals? Haunted handkerchiefs?

As I was fretting over my lack of sophistication, I barely noticed a line of Brigham Young University graduates sharing the same row. Each BYU grad would stand, politely introduce themselves, and start with the same introduction, "Hi, I'm _____, and I'm married." They'd chat about their beautiful wife and children and their mission work. Sequentially, each one upped the ante with humor until the final gentleman ended by reassuring us that there were "no extra wives hidden in closets." The auditorium chuckled en masse.

Then came the guy in the Green Bay Packer hat and Doc Martens boots. Future Hubs stood up, glanced down the row of Married Mormons, and with perfect comedic timing, quipped, "Hi, I'm CJ from Wisconsin. I'm not married yet." He took a long pause. "But I'm certainly *lookin'!*" With eyes twinkling, he raised one eyebrow and smirked. The crowd broke out in raucous laughter.

It was a welcome reprieve from the nervousness of the first day. Especially when a female student from several rows behind him remarked that she was "most definitely *not* looking" and shot a dark look at CJ.

Several hours later, we were in the middle of an alternative universe, performing a physical exam on an inanimate "patient." We followed directions and temporarily ignored the human silhouette in the black vinyl bag resting on each lab table. Instead, all 125 pairs of tense hands palpated the stainless steel surface in front of each of us as we unanimously agreed on our first diagnosis that the tables were very much *not* alive.

The professor's bushy eyebrows knit together as he continued, "There is an inherent need for osteopathic physicians to palpate the life force. The *flow.* The *heat.* The *pulse.* The vibrant *aliveness.*" He paused. The air felt denser, cooler.

"This is ultimately what we seek as physicians: *life,*" he stated emphatically, stopping mid stride between tables.

Our solemn heads bobbled in synchronized agreement.

He pivoted on his heel, making a sound like gritty sandpaper on the floor. He continued his wandering trek in the opposite direction. "Your hands are your tools. Of discernment. Of healing. Over these next few years, we will help you grow these abilities." He seemed to glow with purpose.

"Your training begins today as you carefully respect the life that once inhabited the body before you in the black bag."

Oxygen was sucked from the room as our eyes turned to the body bags resting atop each table. The only sound came from the industrial wall clock.

Tick...tick...tick...

"You must remember this body—though inanimate like the table underneath it—was very much alive once. Its lungs had breath...its muscles had movement...its mind had goals, dreams, and a history. Most of all, this person had generosity. As you explore this most thoughtful gift, please remember to honor and appreciate this person before you. This person marks the start of your journey to heal thousands and thousands within your lifetime."

Tick...tick...tick...

"One final thing. Remember this: In life, we don't have friends. We don't have enemies. We only have teachers. This person had a name. A family. A purpose. As you meet your teacher, it's perfectly normal to have feelings and emotions bubble up. Please treat your classmates with grace and understanding, as we all have a unique relationship with death—forged by experiences in our cultures and families. You may now unzip the bag."

I looked to my lab partners, but no one volunteered for this duty. I grasped the zipper and pulled the tab slowly, tracing over the contour of the wrinkled forehead and down the crooked nose until his face was fully revealed.

We stood there for a moment and absorbed the magnitude of this tradition of educating young physicians with dead bodies. Our classmates went right to work, carving delicate skin, but my anatomy lab group was unique. Before piercing the skin with a scalpel, we felt this undeniable need to anchor this experience. He needed a name and a life story first.

We studied the gray stubble that blanketed his jawline over his downturned mouth. Despite the dehydration of the formaldehyde, his muscles appeared toned and defined. Calloused fingers extended from his wide palms. His large frame reached beyond the table perimeter.

The five of us agreed to name our cadaver Jacques Pierre. We didn't know what happened in his first life, but in this second one, he was a Canadian lumberjack who helped five medical students learn in the most sacred way.

Most importantly, dissecting Jacques helped us galvanize our expressions into the neutral poker faces we needed for our impending medical careers.

CHAPTER FOUR

THE HOUSE ALWAYS WINS

Past the cadavers, past the dizzying microscope slides, and beyond the thrill of a heartbeat in a stethoscope, our heady crush had worn off on this new love interest. I settled into the mundane routine of life with my other medical-student classmates. Like an endless poker game, we were accustomed to rounds and rounds of unscrupulous cards. Final exams, oral quizzes, block testing dealt to us month after month. It seemed the house had the advantage.

Like any good poker tournament, we all developed our lucky habits to increase our confidence at winning. It didn't matter how illogical or silly. If I got one cycle of REM sleep from 3 a.m. to 6 a.m., then chugged my sixteen-ounce Mr. Pibb, donned my lucky fleece, and brought four sharpened pencils, I would get at least an 88 percent on the test every time.

It was day two of the grueling family medicine boards examination. I joined the rest of the bleary-eyed students as we reappeared in the stately hotel conference room. Wearing yoga pants and hoodies, with pockets full of earplugs, we personified ICD-10 41.0 (paroxysmal episodic anxiety). With my hair piled into a ponytail, I was ready to pour gray matter into bubbled sheets.

No poker game had ever had security checkpoints that rigorous. Fingerprints, ID, and adrenaline were required to enter.

A two-day examination like that one guaranteed extra security precautions. Backpacks were not allowed, and bathroom breaks were closely monitored. Bladders of steel recommended. I took one last glance at the metabolic Krebs cycle scribbled on my note card and tried desperately to emboss this into my retinas before shoving it into my backpack. I grabbed my pencils and an unrecognizable driver's license featuring some dewy, fresh-faced, smiling person. Funny how time, stress, and relationships change a person.

Silence was thick. Tension was suffocating. We were standing outside the locked auditorium doors for the second day. Everyone was in their own preparatory lock-and-load mode, a fair-trade Colombian blend of somber and panic. Suddenly, the bolts unlocked and the doors swung wide. We began streaming into the assembly hall, ceremoniously launching empty coffee cups into the trash bin at the entrance. Cup after cup, lofting high in the air. Symbolic gestures of our final gulp. We were eager to finish what we started the day before.

The overhead announcement blared: "*We will start the exam in five minutes. Remember to sit in the* same seat *we assigned you from yesterday.*"

I stepped again through the familiar corals of long tables and found row eleven. I shuffled through, counting seats until I reached seat twenty-three. I was proud that my brain was still able to perform simple addition.

A strained, sweaty student was occupying *my* assigned seat. His neurotic recipe was a carefully arranged fort of pencils spanning the perimeter of his space. He was motionless, hands on his lap, breathing deep, eyes closed. I tiptoed to his side, unsure of how best to break the moment. I paused a few respectful seconds and looked around. The murmur of everyone else settling in put me on edge.

"*We will start the exam in **two** minutes. Please take your seats now,*" the mic blared.

I gently tapped his shoulder, and he jolted to life from my electric fingertip. He hurled a fiery glance at my face. I winced at the burn.

"I'm sorry to interrupt, but I think you have the wrong seat," I declared.

He guarded his pencil fort protectively and sneered in my direction. I was aware of the silence growing as earplugs were shoved into ears and the sound of chairs moving quieted before the test began.

I squeaked, "You're supposed to sit in the same seat as *yesterday*."

His skin drained of all remaining color and his lower lip trembled.

"Yessssterday?" He said the word as if he was learning it for the first time, allowing his tongue to form the syllables carefully. "Wait...*yes-ter-day*? I thought the exam started *today*?"

I gasped involuntarily as I realized his error along with him. Looking for shelter, I found nothing to hide behind, only the collective beams of six pairs of eyeballs around us, witnessing this abomination unfold. Tears brimmed in his eyes and he swept up his pencil fort, fleeing the scene in a blur of sorrow.

With all the ways it can go wrong, it's amazing more of us don't fold our cards during our medical careers. One could say the same about any relationship. Instead, we shuffle the deck and deal again.

What keeps us going?

It's the same answer for any mystery in life: love.

Love keeps us playing the game.

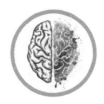

CHAPTER FIVE

I WANT MY FIFTY DOLLARS

We were all new doctors. Interns huddled around the cafeteria table, in the middle of our hospital day. Those focus groups were wrong; doctors *can* agree on one thing. Sitting there, five out of five doctors would all acknowledge that the worst relationship we ever had was with a pager.

Whenever two or more doctors are gathered, you could point a gloved finger at any of them and they'd fit one of three stages in their pager tryst:

1. Pre-call (holding their breath, about to start their exciting twenty-four-hour pager date)

2. On-call (nervous because this pager is hot and could interrupt any second)

3. Post-call (exhausted from all-night pager action)

That day, we were banded together as comrades in the boot camp called Internship, a rite of passage where we practiced our fledgling doctor skills under close supervision. During our breaks, we strengthened our morale with entertaining stories.

One particularly bitter full moon, someone calculated the hours we worked and estimated the take-home pay was $1.50 per hour. Hurtful humor was our shamefully dark bitcoin, exchanged for all those years of sacrificing a social life, marriage, or child-bearing for a penny salary. Nothing was off limits. The pagers clipped to our waists were evidence that we had *seen things*. And we would see a lot more before our boot camp was finished.

Our lifeblood was sharing stories of gory surgical abscesses and impossible feats of survival over a chicken sandwich. Our currency was laughter. Laughter helped us ease the pain. Our depth of knowledge expanded, as did the complexity of our stories, often settling into the legendary lore passed to future medical interns.

That day's topic was pitched by our comrade, as he spent his month on a rotation in the emergency room. Between bites, he asked: "What's the most bizarre thing you've ever extracted from a living human body?"

We *lived* for polls like this. Random nouns filled the air. Raisin. Sandwich. Lightbulb. Screwdriver. Pearl necklace. LEGO. Toothbrush. Barbie doll. A1 Steak Sauce bottle. Gerbil. Sock. Cucumber. Pack of Wrigley's spearmint gum. Wad of fifty-dollar bills.

We were howling as crumbs spewed from our mouths like confetti.

Suddenly, the hospital CEO strolled into the lounge, and a respectful hush descended. We whimpered with suppressed laughter and wiped tears with scratchy cafeteria napkins.

Then it was my turn.

"Today's poll is inspired by morning rounds with Dr. Calder," I announced.

There was a collective groan.

Everyone despised Dr. Calder, a notoriously unyielding doctor with an astringent bedside manner. Known for slinging impossible trivia to the unsuspecting intern, he slashed their confidence with his snide comments. He drank their tears in his morning tea. In fact, there was a dedicated alcove on the third floor which provided discreet cover for weeping interns to blow their noses or drip Visine in red eyes. This became known as Calder Corner.

"What are the strangest orders you've ever written for a patient?" I asked.

They chewed thoughtfully.

Then they answered with a litany of phrases that sounded much like requests for a touring rock band:

"Remove all Jello from food tray before entering room."
"Dispense one beer to nursery. Open can and pour into water for baby's first bath."
"Keep door closed per patient request. Knock five times before entering."

"I have a new winner today," I proclaimed. "I was writing orders to discharge a sweet, ninety-four-year-old, demented male back to the nursing home, and what do you think he requested to have from the hospital staff before heading back to his facility?"

They put forth suggestions: Whisky on the rocks. Candy. Steak dinner. Motorcycle.

"He requested...a hand job!" I chuckled and blushed. "So I turned to Dr. Calder and asked if he wanted me to write for this to be administered twice or three times daily."

Guffaws of uncontrollable laughter erupted.

Story by story, this was how we fought against inevitable exhaustion. When our primary relationship was with a pager, we had to find joy in the moments of humanity.

The CEO shook his head and slammed the door behind him, the doorknob rattling emphatically.

CHAPTER SIX

YO MOMMA

A decade later, I was the one rattling another doorknob. This time, the loose knob belonged to my own kitchen pantry. It was 2 p.m. on a Saturday afternoon (which equates to 10 p.m. in working-doctor-mom time). I had successfully played all my cards in the game of medical school and advanced to the round of matrimony and motherhood.

I was lost in the middle of an intense game of Pantry Tetris: unpack the grocery bags with one hand, stack food with the other. Trying to find a vacant slot in my pantry that was the exact size of a Quaker oatmeal box or six-pack of applesauce was supremely tricky in a pantry that always smelled of a stray onion I could never locate. Putting away groceries for my family of five had become a tradition of *sniff*—stack—*sniff*—stack.

My kitchen island was a mountain of packages, and I was a heap of fatigue.

"Hey, Mom?" my oldest, Owen, piped up between mouthfuls of granola. He paused, allowing his seven-year-old mind to carefully assemble his next remark. "Does God keep secrets?"

"Of course. He's the best guy around to keep them." I felt the sizzle of my Momtuition warning me that a moment was upon us and I needed to focus. I extracted my head from deep behind the shelves. I would never find that onion. I added, "But, of course, if it's a secret *that can hurt someone*, it's best to tell a grown-up so they can help."

"Okay," his seven-year-old mind was temporarily satisfied.

Emery, my five-year-old daughter, quietly surveyed the room with her bright hazel eyes as she swallowed her peanut butter and jelly sandwich.

For a brief moment, I'd proudly silenced the pagers on my motherhood belt.

An electric silence followed, punctuated by granola munching. I resumed onion reconnaissance and pantry balancing. Our toddler, Beckett, scooted on the ground, clearing debris like a chunky human Roomba with his marshmallow knees.

Without warning, Emery's sandwich clattered onto the plate. Her eyes bounced upward, fixated toward the ceiling. Her five-year-old mouth fell open, glossy pink petal lips forming an "O" shape.

We stared at her.

After an eternity, her gaze slowly drifted back down. Tiny shoulders popped up into a brief shrug, and then her starfish hands picked up the sandwich again.

She clipped a bite from the crust with hasty intent and turned to her older brother. "I know what your secret is." She swallowed victoriously.

I closed the fridge just in time to witness the white panic flash across my son's face.

"NO, YOU DON'T! THERE'S NO WAY," he barked. His fist pounded the table.

Emery smirked proudly, eyebrows lifted. She chewed with increased gusto.

Owen's body vibrated with rage. "YOU'RE LYING. NO WAY. HOW?"

"I just asked God. He *told* me." Her steely eyes challenged his.

My son exploded out of his chair and deployed the standard solution for all bickering and dilemmas: "MOOOM! MOOOOOOM."

As if on cue, my *hospital* pager began chirping. I was on call. Actual call.

"Hey. Hold on—" My words failed to silence the crescendo of battle. My daughter was a calm statue at the table, my son a whirling dervish.

He continued, "FINE. If He told you...WHAT'S MY SECRET,THEN?!" Tiny arms folded in front of his puffed chest.

I pressed the button to silence my pager and waited. I was more curious about this outcome than what the hospital operator might have had for me.

Emery sighed deeply, rolled her eyes, and shook her head. Her fringe bangs swung back and forth as she let out an exaggerated chuckle. "I can't tell you."

Owen was livid. "WHY?!"

"BECAUSE. *IT'S. A. SECRET.*"

All the "nonviolent confrontation" training in medical school didn't prepare me for motherhood. In residency, you sling a belt full of pagers, ready for action. Responsible for dozens of human lives with a white coat of impervious armor. If something bad happens, you can call a code and people appear from *everywhere* to *voluntarily help you.*

There's a corresponding code for everything, each hospital slightly different:

> Code blue (cardiac arrest)
> Code red (fire)
> Code pink (infant abduction)
> Code brown (someone ate a three-bean taco and left evidence hanging in the air)

No matter the code, unfamiliar staff you've *never met* will hear the distress signal and *voluntarily sprint to your exact location* and help you. No questions asked. Calling a "code white to room 305" meant there was an unruly and combative patient that needed physical restraint. Burly security guards and ER staff would hurdle over carts and sprint up three flights of stairs like an ultimate hospital obstacle course. It was the closest to modern-day chivalry you'll ever experience, and the biggest disappointment in preparation for parenting.

This does *not* happen in motherhood.

I should've known. As a little girl, I avoided playing "house" in kindergarten class. I didn't see the fun in carrying a baby doll around on one hip while preparing plastic dinner on a plastic stove with a missing plastic knob. The diaper was always falling off, and the food was always the same: purple grapes and yellow corn on a wooden plate. Everyone exaggerated their bites and cooed, "Mmmm" until the teacher announced the end of free time.

Instead of imitating reality, I preferred to play with transformation. Long before *Extreme Makeover* on HGTV, I yearned to improve something, like the afternoon I outfitted my tiny dollhouse with construction paper slides and yarn pulleys attached to matchbox elevators. Masking tape was everywhere.

I desperately wanted to live in this rehabilitated dollhouse. I became quite obsessed. I'd stoop down and peer in the window, imagining what it would be like to walk on the felt rug and climb the plastic stairs. Thankfully, my father knew how to make this happen.

"Daddy, is there any way I can shrink my body to fit inside here?" I remember pleading with him, turning to showcase my utopia.

"Wow, that's pretty...*spectacular*," he remarked.

That wasn't enough for me. I followed him around all afternoon with my move-in-ready dollhouse, asking how I could shrink to get inside and experience those twenty-thread-count sheets.

After several hours of begging, he finally revealed the secret, "You know how chewing and swallowing a vitamin will make your body grow bigger? Well, it turns out that if you just suck on the vitamin *without swallowing*, it's the reverse! Your body will shrink instead of grow!"

Of course. How could my six-year-old brain have missed the obvious?

I positioned the dollhouse directly beside the living room couch, angled perfectly in anticipation of leaping my three-inch pixie body onto the upper attic roof.

My dad dropped the Flintstone vitamin into my eager palm. I carefully placed it on my tongue and laid down on the couch. Eyes closed. Giddy but unmoving. Minutes passed.

Every time my dad walked by, I'd ask a new question about the process. "Do I need to close my eyes?" (No.) "How long does this take?" (It depends on the season. Shrinking is slower in summer.) "Do all vitamins do this?" (Only the orange Flintstone vitamins in Lot # 3622. It was a special batch.)

When I'd had enough, I'd mumble through the disintegrating vitamin on my tongue and ask, "Am I smaller yet?"

My dad would walk over, extend his arms from my head to toes, and proclaim, "*Yes*! I can see you've shrunk a little already!" This would encourage me to stay the course. I'd gaze lovingly at the red construction paper slide extending down the dollhouse stairs and return to my supine position.

Soon.

Eventually, the vitamin dissolved and it was determined that I didn't shrink *enough* that day. My dad encouraged me to repeat this process every day, but somehow I lost interest. He was a brilliantly imaginative man who knew how to instill the awe of possibility and wonder. Which balanced perfectly with my mother's skepticism and tendency to question everything.

As I grew older, I assumed I was not the maternal type because I preferred to explore the land of make-believe and human physiology instead of dishes and diapers.

And then the invitation to reconsider who you think you are happens when you least expect it. I found mine in the hazel eyes of CJ during a study break in the first few months of medical school. We were supposed to be reviewing the anatomical muscles of the arm, bent over a copy of *Netter*. He was pointing at the brachioradialis, but I was secretly admiring his biceps. Wrong muscle, but I didn't care. A plate of fries separated us.

"Do you think there's such a thing as soulmates?" he asked, picking up a crunchy fry.

I paused. I wasn't sure, but I felt something pulling me forward to this moment.

"Yes, I think so. What about you?"

"I think we do, but not just one. I think we can have many. A soulmate is someone we connect with instantly and effortlessly," he replied.

And that's exactly the moment when I knew. I wanted to experience my *own* transformation to marriage and motherhood. Brushing off salt from my fingers, I was suddenly curious how it would feel to have a baby on my hip. Between two smart and sassy doctors-to-be, we could certainly create some amazing humans together...

How hard could it be? Motherhood was simply about tending to a growing garden of people, right? Kindergarten taught me everything I needed to know. Just keep feeding them dinner, they'll go "Mmm" and run off to play for hours in the backyard. They'll scrape their knees, you'll put real Band-Aids on, and crying will stop immediately.

When they grow older, they'll become helpful, mini-roommates. Explain how to run the laundry machine once, and they'll fall in love with "playing house" for real because they appreciate keeping a tidy home, right? They'll always heed your warnings about wearing bike helmets and never forget to apply sunscreen. They're made directly from your own shared DNA, so they'll think just like you. All you need are hugs and love, right?

I was wrong.

Wrong on many levels, but especially about the missing ingredient to motherhood.

It took a decade before I needed the critical ingredient of caffeine. Drinking ground bean water didn't appeal to me ever since one memorable 8 a.m. Biology 201 session when a classmate felt the need to lean in and whisper something with such pungent coffee breath that my eyelashes melted completely off. I haven't had lush lashes ever since.

I made it through college, medical school, an internship, and residency without the crutch of coffee. I could rally my body to stay up for thirty-six hours straight to learn how to drain an abscess. I could shake off heavy weariness and power through hours of exam testing. I could stay awake to catch another baby on the labor-and-delivery floor while carrying my own inside. No caffeine required.

Until our second child, Emery, was born.

The combustible stress of adding a newborn into the mix of toddler potty training with a full-time doctor career was *unprecedented*. In my postpartum fog, I figured this dilemma could only be helped in two ways: befriend a member of the local cocaine drug cartel or find an additional wife. Coffee was the logical third choice.

Motherhood attaches an invisible pager to your belt. Forever. At any moment, it'll signal your attention to: find the yellow permission slip, explain why primates make tears, unclog the toilet without a plunger, or dissect a cookie into equal parts in height, width, and nanogram weight.

Strangely, the battery on this motherhood pager never needs replacing. There's no way to silence it. Motherhood duty is 24/7 without benefits of being "post-call," and never allowing a moment of comatose napping. No mandated work-hour restrictions exist. No vacations. You show up every day: sick, tired, grumpy.

Yes, my invitation to consider motherhood arrived when I was distracted by a bulging bicep and a plate of fries. But I didn't show up for the real party until one cold October morning in

2002 when we brought our first newborn, Owen, home from the hospital.

Still in his car seat, I carefully placed this squirmy pile of flesh in the middle of the living room floor, his bulging torso secured firmly with the five-point harness. Right at that moment, that baby was pristine and perfect. Nothing had tarnished his body or soul. No mistakes had been made. He was a human blank canvas.

I stared down at him. His saucer eyes stared up at me. He knew. He could see I had no idea what to do next. Suddenly, I panicked at this blank space.

With our bundle of joy still parked in the center of our room, CJ and I collapsed on the futon. But it felt different. This was a well-worn lumpy college futon from our first apartment, and normally it felt comfortable. Yet, somehow during the hospital stay, it had transformed into a dangerous threat with razor-sharp corners. Our coffee table also sprouted equally pointed edges ready to pluck out an eyeball. It seemed our whole home underwent a powerful remodel, and everything was an ominous threat.

We watched him for a moment, gurgling and happy, safely tucked in his car seat. We looked at each other.

Now what?

And just like that, one moment I was rocking a colicky baby at 3 a.m., pat-pat-patting their little diaper butt, and the next, I was handing over the car keys.

Modern motherhood requires extraordinary skills that our ancestors couldn't prepare us for. Our ancestors didn't spend hours with unblinking eyes, staring at YouTube for hours trying to learn common core math to help their children complete two sheets of homework. They didn't have to calculate the number of licks it would take to get to the center of the toxic lead toy from China. They didn't lie awake at night wondering who ThiccBoi is and why they "friend requested" their preteen daughter.

Instead, motherhood is one long, time-pressured fetching game, built on a crumbling memory. Like a contestant on a game show, you find yourself in ridiculous situations. It's 7:10 a.m. The bus is pulling up at your door and you have ninety seconds. Can *you* find the location of that one orange hair scrunchie?! Hurry: bake a dozen cookies for tomorrow's Star Student of the Week celebration, find the lost library book, and assemble remnants of an incomplete eighties costume for Spirit Week.

The spontaneity and creativity needed in motherhood challenges any diligent medical student, who has spent decades carefully choosing every fork in the road. Instead, motherhood goes beyond the forks. Motherhood throws open the whole cutlery drawer, launching spoons, knives, chopsticks, old hot sauce packets, and screwdrivers to the ground. Just when you assemble it back together, a fight breaks out from your kids in the kitchen about who has the *bigger* spoon and *better* fork.

Meanwhile, you use the screwdriver to tighten that loose pantry doorknob.

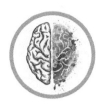

CHAPTER SEVEN

THE DOORKNOB QUESTION

It was Friday! The best day of the week—for most *other* industries. As a physician, with over a decade in primary care, Fridays meant my patients suddenly remembered they needed their prescription refilled. Fridays reminded them that it was time to make that urgent appointment for the mysterious chronic toe pain that's lasted four years.

With the advent of electronic medical records and a click of a few keys, patients can send messages instantly to my inbox, requesting urgent intervention. If I don't answer within a few hours, all malpractice attorneys start salivating in the tri-state area. This convenient ease of technology has created a constant drip of ill-prepared, last-minute patient hysteria that fuels my undercurrent of dissatisfaction. Drafting permission letters for a service pet unicorn. Waiting on hold for the third appeal for insurance coverage on a generic prescription.

"Give it to me, doc," Harry muttered with a twinkle in his eye. "Will I be sitting on the toilet for the next week?"

My hands danced over the keyboard as I kept one eye on Harry and the other on my computer screen. File this skill under "Things They Don't Teach You in Med School," subchapter "How to Effectively Type While Appearing Attentive During a Medical Appointment."

At that moment, my patient, Harry, was referring to the inevitable diarrhea that would occur with his antibiotic prescription. He was added to my overbooked schedule for a sore throat. His rapid strep test was negative, but it was Friday and it had been an exhausting week. By that time, any noble responsibility as a public health servant had escaped my soul. I was no longer worried about global antibiotic resistance. I just want to get home by 5 p.m.

My nurse's head popped from behind the door just as the sound of retching began in the next exam room. "Dr. Salyer, your patient in room three didn't handle that injection very well. And the other patient in room four wants to know how much longer you will be."

I pinned the corners of my mouth into a polite smile and nodded in her direction. I finished Harry's discharge recommendations in haste. I compromised and explained he should try supportive care *first*, and only if it worsens, should he fill the antibiotic prescription. I proclaimed the benefits of throat lozenges, danger signs to watch for (swelling, fever, difficulty swallowing, divine hallucinations, table dancing, whatever). He agreed quietly.

Too quietly. Almost a whisper.

My intuition prickled.

I rose from the stool and walked to the door as vomiting from the other room crescendoed. Just as my hand made contact with the doorknob, Harry's words launched into the air, "Actually, the *real reason* I made this appointment..."

The dreaded Doorknob Question.

"Should I be concerned if I've had *crushing chest pain* since last night?" Harry muttered.

Doorknob Questions happen when patients cloak their request for a medical appointment in false packaging. Denial is a comfortable fleece hoodie worn by fear. It's scary to say things out loud to a receptionist. I forget that as physicians, we live in the land of physiology and disease. Complex diagnoses and dramatic symptoms are our native language. We shun the adage "ignorance is bliss," and instead, we keep poking and digging to find clarity. It can feel jarring and unnerving to most people that are fearful of what their body might be broadcasting.

It's easier for a patient to deny their chest pain, embarrassing genital sores, or evaporating memory loss in favor of a cute sore throat or generic cough. The front desk prefers this, too. They'll gleefully schedule that "quick appointment," and strategically place it in the crowded lineup, unaware of this impending catastrophe that will delay the entire afternoon. Sometimes, a patient will endure radiation from chest x-rays, gag from throat swabs, or subject themselves to whatever is requested just to guarantee time with the doctor. I don't blame them. It's weeks to gain a spot in front of most family doctors.

Maybe it's not a problem of supply or demand. Maybe we just need more of those enchanted doorknobs installed. Once my hand touches it, the real motive behind their visit is magically revealed. Perhaps if we all were honest in the beginning, we could get meaningful work done faster. Every politician needs doorknobs like these.

Within a few minutes, Harry was strapped to an EKG machine and sent to our local hospital for further evaluation. Thankfully, he only had a severe case of indigestion.

I sat back at my desk, reflecting on this mathematical relationship. The number of Doorknob Questions seemed to rise in direct proportion to full moons, Fridays, and minutes ticking toward 5 p.m.

It was only 11:30 a.m.

CHAPTER EIGHT

I LOVE YOU, MIHALY

The morning was finished. The lobby emptied, and I heard the last patient's shoe squeaking across the linoleum. This was my cue to tie running shoes to my own feet. I slipped through the back door of the clinic and began my daily escape. There was something about this methodical pounding of the sidewalk.

Perhaps colic is a lifelong affliction, quelled only by rhythm. The early pat-pat-patting of a baby's back is replaced by another choice later on. Since we all have invisible diapers of existential crap affixed to our collective psyche, only those adults that find a competent rhythm will achieve calm. In my case it was running.

Nothing could be more out of character for me than voluntary physical activity. I was reigning champion of Last Place for my entire K–12 physical educational experience. I had an uncanny ability to forget game rules as soon as my hands touched a ball or bat. Every sport in PE class translated into the same game of "hot potato" in my brain. If a classmate accidentally tossed the ball into my hands out of desperation, my whole world turned to lava. I tried to get rid of this responsibility immediately, even if it meant scoring in the opponent's basket.

How does someone like me voluntarily run during a lunch break?

Motherhood. It's the gateway drug to exploring the unthinkable.

If my first child taught me about unconditional love during colic and my second child introduced me to the world of medium-roast coffee, it was my third, Beckett, that encouraged me to consider new methods of stress relief. With a responsibility of 1,900 patients in my panel, I needed something unthinkable. Something bizarre. Something metaphorical to free my mind.

It started as a simple walk "for fresh air." When walks became mundane, I added challenges because that's just the kind of annoying person I am. The inner Sagittarius lives for milestones and checkpoints. I didn't stop running until I passed five stop signs. Six people on riding mowers. One mile. Two.

Before I knew it, I was *voluntarily* packing my own exercise clothes in a bag every morning. When "exercise" didn't entail wearing the starchy yellow school-issued uniform or humiliation of being picked last, I didn't mind it. I actually *looked forward* to it. I always seemed to have a slight buzz afterward, and my afternoons felt easier.

I knew something magical was happening after one pivotal three-mile run. I felt electric. My brain was churning through ideas and epiphanies. I solved a mysterious diagnosis plaguing one of my patients. I wrote a poem. As I ran past flowers, butterflies, and clouds in the sky, I felt my inner Carl Sagan connecting to the "star stuff" of the universe.

I was getting hooked on something bigger than myself.

Research by psychologist Mihaly Csikszentmihalyi explained that being "in flow" meant full immersion in an activity with complete absorption and a loss of time passing. All senses are engaged, and the ego dissolves. These daily runs were giving me a healthy dose of flow I hadn't felt in years.

In kindergarten, it happened when my greasy hands were spreading orange finger paint across rough construction paper, and I couldn't hear my teacher announce it was time to clean up. In middle school, it was when I was lost for several hours in a high-stakes game of *Super Mario Bros.* and forgot to drink a single glass of water. In college, it was hours of dancing, flannel shirt tied around my waist, lost in the throbbing music of La Bouche in a smoky club.

Research from Steven Kotler's Flow Genome Project shows that your brain releases feel-good neurotransmitters[1] during flow state such as norepinephrine, dopamine, anandamide, and serotonin. It's practically medicinal. I hadn't felt this in a long time. No wonder I was hooked.

I was prescribing my own daily flow.

I rounded the final corner of my noon run. My feet thumping the pavement and my brain floating. Transformation nearly complete. No matter how fast or slow, I'm never the same person when I return from a run.

But this run was special. It would be my last run for months. It was my turn to be the patient for a routine surgery.

If there was a World's Strongest Baby competition, my nine-pound offspring would rival Magnus Ver Magnusson in the epic head circumference category. High achievers, breaking all records—and my uterus—in their path of destruction.

Three babies later, it was determined that my uterus was no longer "CrossFit." It became an anatomical mascot of my exhaustion as a working doctor mom: stubborn and droopy. As a holistic osteopathic doctor, I originally pledged to keep all organs till death do us part. However, if a partial hysterectomy guaranteed burpees at the gym without potty breaks, then all I needed to know was which dotted line to sign.

Getting off the treadmill of a busy family medicine career rarely happens, and if removing my uterus was the golden ticket of admission, I was ready. I scheduled this to coincide with the Thanksgiving holiday because it seemed appropriate—laying on a table with hands stuffed where the sun doesn't shine. Why should turkeys have all the fun?

CHAPTER NINE
BLOODY MARY

A week later and a few pounds lighter, I was basting the golden turkey after it roasted all morning. We both made it through the stuffing. This was the only task I was allowed in my postoperative state. Being a patient was frustrating. This "vacation" required a new interdependence I was not used to. Each time I asked someone to lift something heavier than ten pounds, I felt a tiny backward step in my composure. No wonder it's called "patient."

The sound of holiday dinner preparations from CJ and our extended family hummed around me: murmuring conversations, dishes clanking, and toddler feet stuttering. Little fingers were folding napkins into neat triangles, and autumn centerpieces were adjusted and fluffed.

I retreated to the master bathroom one final time before our feast. As I was washing my hands, I heard a "pop." I paused at the cute sound. Short and staccato. It sounded exactly like the seam of your leggings snapping after a low squat, or a cool water balloon breaking on a hot, steamy sidewalk.

But instead of something cool and refreshing, there was a river of warmth streaming from between my legs.

I glanced down. Vibrant red arterial blood.

I was hemorrhaging.

My mind jumped to First Aid 101: put pressure on a bleeding wound. But...how would one put pressure on *this*?! I grabbed a terry cloth towel and sat down on the floor.

I watched silently as the rounded scarlet edge of blood inched painlessly across the textured linoleum.

That awful linoleum. During our home tour years prior, I pointed to this floor and announced to the real estate agent, "*That's* definitely the first thing to go." A horrid reminder of the equally disastrous nineties decor trends, that pale linoleum inspired the unrealistic optimism belonging to a mother of two. I assumed I'd have unlimited hours to spend remodeling this home while my two children would play silently in the lush— and freshly mowed—backyard. They'd be so busy collecting bugs in their pristine seersucker overalls that they'd only interrupt me to ask for help pouring a reasonably small glass of lightly sweetened lemonade. The real estate agent had nodded in affirmation to my daydream.

I had no clue of the changes coming with the time-warp whiplash that would happen when I added a third baby in my arms. Fast-forward, and this linoleum was mocking me with its indignant beigeness. It made a great blank canvas for blood, though.

As a doctor, I'm keenly aware of the standard risks of infection, hemorrhage, and death with any routine surgery. But as a *patient*, I mindlessly scribbled my signature on the informed consent a week prior, giving no thought.

I watched the blood spread farther.

My brain spat forth a series of random suggestions from decades of grade-school assemblies held in sweaty gymnasiums:

STOP, DROP, ROLL?
TAKE COVER IN A HEAVY BASEMENT BATHTUB?
CALL POISON CONTROL?

Nope.

I slumped to the floor to lie flat on my back. I remained motionless. My eyeballs strained as I watched the border of my crimson fluid creep along the ugly beigeness.

My brain continued fighting with itself. Thoughts were tangled in a judo match for dominance: survival or trivia. Wasn't there a sale on flooring at Home Depot? *Will it cost extra to have them remove blood-stained linoleum?* How many units of blood before I feel a heart attack or stroke? *Is it five? Can you present the answer in a multiple-choice format?*

When that proved futile, my mind explored solutions with a side of denial. What would be the most effective ways to disguise this blood-soaked towel and continue with the festivities: Bright red clown costume? Vintage hoop skirt? Maybe this was a time to outsource some help. Certainly my clever husband would have had ideas.

Ever since the first day I met CJ, he was full of ideas, long before I knew he was my Future Husband. With ideas rooted in humor, he could dispense laughter to alleviate any dire situation.

My favorite memory happened when our class was learning how to interpret x-rays. Over one hundred medical students were squeezed into a dim basement laboratory room, holding films that captured x-ray versions of our individual postures.

Slowly slipping our films from their envelope jacket, we hung each on the darkened view boxes. With the last film clicked securely in place, our professor shut off the overhead lights and activated the light boxes. Instantly, we were encased by the illumination of cold, gray spines on all four walls. As we stood in front of our own images, we recognized our familiar body shapes.

Then the room fell silent.

And a collective gasp broke the air when we realized what was happening.

Turns out, x-rays reveal a lot more than calcified skeletons. Nestled within each bony portrait was the soft curves of skin folds. And within those folds, a more intimate portrait emerged: the contours of our classmates' breasts, hips, and pubic mounds.

The awkward silence grew tense as our eyes wandered.

Out of nowhere, Future Hubs quipped, "Man. I should've *prepped* a bit before they took this picture—if you know what I mean." He grimaced and winked.

Laughter cascaded through the room.

That was exactly the kind of medicine I needed as I sat bleeding on my bathroom floor: humor. I needed to know everything would be fine and this was just another crazy plot twist in our sitcom of raising three kids in rural Wisconsin. I summoned CJ with my politest phone voice and waited in anticipation.

I tried to guess what masterpiece he'd comment on first. Bloody Rorschach tests? Turkey basting gone wrong?

His smile appeared in the doorway and promptly dissolved into a hasty four-letter word. Then, he vanished.

Wait. Doctors *never* panic.

Unless you're a doctor and you see *another* doctor panic. As terror choked my throat, my younger sister materialized by my side, doing her best to distract and uplift. Growing up around our grandpa's funeral home, we honed our skills to deal out macabre comments like a professional blackjack player. We doubled down on death like experts. There was no level of perilous conversations that we couldn't handle.

She started with the simple stuff. Top methods to remove stubborn blood stains. Best song to play at funerals. We quickly graduated to more ghastly topics. Serial killers. Techniques of dismemberment and disposal. Methods of proper haunting so she knew I was still around.

"Compost me or plant me in a tree pod," I requested. "Maybe turn my ashes into a vinyl record that plays Alanis Morissette's 'Hand In My Pocket.'"

"*Isn't it ironic?*" she sang.

"Don't cha think?" I chuckled. "My epitaph could read: 'The uterus, the very life-giving anatomical organ, was her ultimate downfall.'"

My banter softened as tears welled in my eyes. I witnessed fear flicker across my sister's unflappable face.

Silence is a rare treat, with exception of two conditions: when a toddler is in the next room, or when you run out of distracting comedy material during your hemorrhage.

As EMS carried my gurney down the front-porch stairs, my watery eyes landed on the round, sweet faces of my three children. Their velvety cheeks glistening wet with tears. I absorbed every detail: the sausage fingers of two-year-old Beckett gripping his well-worn flannel blanket, ten-year-old Owen holding a colorful LEGO house he just built, and eight-year-old Emery in her Sunday's best—a smoothly ironed, expressionless face. I wondered if she'd become a pathologist with that level of effortless stoicism.

I rolled past each child, assuring them that everything would be *fine*. That four-letter word of adulthood. Everything is *fine*. Yet, everything was clearly *not* fine.

I wanted nothing more at that moment to download all the volumes of love I have for them into each millisecond kiss. I worried their only memories of Mom would be a stressed doctor, collapsing every evening from fatigue. In each peck of their cheeks, I tried to transmit all my thoughts so they knew—without a doubt—that their frazzled mom deeply cared for them.

In my world, *everything was meaningful and important*. I couldn't ever "gloss over" anyone or anything. I am a mom incapable of gloss.

Toddler Beckett was first. I squeezed his soft hand, pressing my memories into his palm. All those afternoons, speeding to daycare just so I could pick him up five minutes earlier. All those hours, humming a repurposed tune from Finnish summer camp as I cradled him to sleep in my arms, ignoring a perpetually cluttered house without regret. All those moments when I felt his wonderment and wisdom, like he existed for centuries before ending up in my lap. His soul had a familiarity to me unlike any other.

Next was Owen, our first born. In my momentary gaze, I tried to burn my love into his retinas with my stare. I showed him the pride I felt as he taught himself how to ride a bike. I remembered the admiration I felt as he assembled a detailed Powerpoint presentation to support his request to purchase *Halo* on Xbox. Or his fearless ability to make the audience laugh during a grade-school lip-synch performance. I would never worry that he couldn't take care of himself.

Finally, my daughter, Emery. Her birth was the only time I cried during labor and delivery. Special tears that represented my extremes of elation and despair at raising a confident daughter in an unjust world. Like a porcupine, she was both adorably self-aware and—at times—tricky to hug. She entered the world from a mystical plane, wearing an invisible backpack preloaded with boldness and fearlessness beyond her years. I wanted her to know how awestruck I was with her prickly magnificence. She had a personality to fill any room.

The ambulance bolted from our home, and CJ followed in our family car. Within minutes, I felt medical staff crawling over my body, assessing the damage. Trying my best to be a *patient* patient, I didn't ask CJ to interpret what was happening. When a med flight helicopter was summoned, I knew this meant I needed a higher level of care. While they prepared me for transport, he prepared to follow on ground.

Entering the helicopter, I was convinced my Finnish grandmother was behind this masterful design. "There's a place for everything and everything has its place." The organizational skills in the tiny cockpit of essentials was astounding.

Walls were draped with extravagant displays of sterile medical equipment, each piece properly positioned in a puzzle of awe. No wasted space there. The nurse and doctor were clad in bright orange jumpsuits and equally compact. Their employment contract probably limited intake of Oreos per year to guarantee a tiny body mass index. I reminded myself to try and look at the outside of the helicopter next time. Maybe there was a ruler painted beside the door with a warning: "You must be *this* short to ride this ride."

Still strapped to the gurney and unable to talk above the noise, I searched the eyes of the mini-Oompa-Loompa flight staff for answers. Straightforward and silent "thumbs-up" signals were exchanged over clipboards. I was acutely aware that I was straddling the line between mortician and doctor. I needed to ask, *How alive am I? How close to death have I slipped? Tell me.*

I tried to interpret context by analyzing their hands. Was that a fervently rushed scribble on the triplicate paperwork? Was she doodling? Was that an *urgent* or *panicked* "thumbs-up"?

That looked like a calm thumb.

So much adrenaline. It heightens every sensation. I was suddenly aware of a mosquito buzzing in Idaho and the imperceptible change in barometric pressure across the Arctic. I felt it on my chest.

No. Wait. They placed equipment on my chest. IV tubing was unrolled. Bags of fluid swung above my head. My body had become an accessory side table to rest their clipboards.

The impassive nurse placed heavy noise-canceling earphones onto my head right at the moment I was jolted with electric panic.

Levels below the mass of equipment on my body tray, below the gurney straps, below the heavy blankets and towels, I felt my blood seeping through my clothes onto the steel floor.

Cue cortisol-fueled panic. I don't do well with secrets. I need information. *What are they saying? Why are they placing a second large bore IV? What is my blood pressure now? How's my EKG looking? How much longer before I am drained of all blood? Will there be a white light? Who will text CJ to remind him about the wet laundry in the washer?*

My orange tour guides offered no assistance. This was all part of a day in their midflight office. Paper shuffling over my body.

Water cooler talk that I couldn't hear. I had become a part of their corporate-branded decor.

I soaked in their routine choreography like calming rain. I began my silent mantra with that four-letter word: This is all going to be *fine*. I'm *fine*.

FINE.

White light.

CHAPTER TEN

THE NDE PRESCRIPTION

I found myself lost in what appeared to be a pharmacy. I could have been hallucinating. The glaring fluorescent overhead lights were blinding white. I was barefoot and wearing a hospital gown. The aisles were gleamingly empty, but shelves were stocked with magazines, eye drops, and generic ibuprofen. Was I on the last courtesy stop to pick up snacks before standing in the long lines at the pearly gates? I hoped there was a red slide like Chutes and Ladders, allowing last-minute decisions to drift back to Earth.

I sauntered to the check-out window. The aged pharmacist greeted me with expectation. He was holding an orange prescription bottle and already unfolding the package insert with tiny five-point-font text.

"Hi there." He cleared his throat unceremoniously, adjusting his bifocals and peering at my demographics. "I see your doctor prescribed NDE-*lite*. Since the full near-death experience isn't covered by your insurance, NDE-lite is a less-potent version without the long tunnel and choir of angels." His tone was monotonous, most likely from years of repeating the same instructions. His enthusiasm was as dry as his cuticles. His nose hairs whistled with each expiration.

"Fifty percent of individuals who experience an NDE mentioned an awareness of being dead. And 56 percent of those felt it was a positive experience. Thirty-one percent described traveling through a tunnel, and 32 percent spoke of interacting with deceased people."

Saliva pooled in each corner of his mouth. He shuffled the paper and aimed his weathered face at me.

"Since you've never filled this prescription before, let me explain the dosage and side effects. NDE-lite begins working immediately after administration. You will reflect on your utility in relationships, career, family, and goals. Once NDE-lite has worn off (half-life varies with individuals), you will resume normal activities with a renewed perspective." He squinted his bushy eyebrows at the prescription and lifted his glasses temporarily. "It says here, no refills on this prescription unless covered by your insurance."

I was suddenly aware that there was no clock on the wall, and no other employees were visible.

The pharmacist continued, "NDEs can change the trajectory of your life. You'll be able to organize your priorities with more accurate discernment. But research has shown that we don't need extreme situations to glean psychological benefit from them. NDE-lite was designed with the risk/benefit ratio in mind: no prolonged comas or choirs of angels. Each person who receives NDE-lite will gain benefit of some sort."

He dropped his bifocals and leaned forward on his elbow as if whispering a secret. The smell of mothballs ever more pungent as he inched closer. "In fact, my shelves are overflowing with NDE-lite. I wish more doctors were aware of this prescription. It gives the patient a chance to contemplate, instead of clinging to the status quo."

He punched the counter with his meaty fist and I jumped. My hospital gown flapped in the breeze.

"Otherwise, people just keep plugging along at monotony. We don't plan for much growth or reflection. We don't participate in ceremonies or seek vision quests—unless you're a celebrity willing to pay for a personal ayahuasca pilgrimage through muddy Peru," he huffed. This was obviously something he felt strongly about. One of the papers fluttered to the ground behind his counter.

His head dipped below my line of sight. I stood there, arms limp at my sides. I heard his muffled voice from under the counter. "What if we all swallowed an NDE-lite every two years and reflected on the current state of our affairs? Like a planned *soft reset* for our life! What if we made this event just as routine as an employee wellness physical, a class reunion, or renewing the lease on your car? What if we treated our lives with anticipated review?"

He rose up and emphasized his last word by stapling paper corners. He cleared his throat like the motor of a lawn mower. "This could be like a checkpoint in the road with the option to take another lap or veer off to a new course—"

He stopped as if realizing a mistake. His eyes widened and he said abruptly, "I'm sure you know there is a generic substitute for NDE? It's available without prescription."

I shook my head, my bare feet glued to the spot.

His leathery face lifted with delight and he smiled. "The generic version provides the same perspective shift with similar results! You'll experience a wide spectrum of emotions from despair to elation. You'll learn to focus on only what is important. You will excavate love so deep and meaningful, you cannot *even* comprehend it!"

A darkness descended across his white brow and it fell back to its furrowed state. He lowered his tone. "But, the side effects are many. It's not as fast-acting as NDE-lite. Results can vary. Unfortunately, it also has a very long half-life, which makes it an unpopular choice. Potency is somewhat diluted, so many don't even realize the benefit of this life-changing effect." He paused long enough to notice my rapt gaze.

His eyes blinked knowingly. "It's called motherhood."

CHAPTER ELEVEN
I'M NOT DEAD YET

My eyes fluttered open. The walls of the pharmacy had been replaced with the trauma bay.

"So, do you have any kids?" the trauma nurse asked sweetly into my ear. She was bent down over me, as I was still strapped to the gurney.

Motherhood. Tears splintered from my eyes and burned down the sides of my face. I was lying in an unfamiliar emergency room, yearning for the unconsciousness of anesthesia.

"Can you *please* sedate me?" I pleaded. Anything to quiet the fear in my brain's amygdala. Asking about motherhood was like tickling my Achilles' heel. It was my biggest weakness.

Her voice softened. "Oh, honey. You know we can't do that. Too risky. Your blood pressure would plummet even further if we did." She taped additional IV tubing to my wrist. "We're just waiting for the surgeon to come down and figure out what happened."

My eyes studied the electrocardiogram machine to my right. Like a glowing economic recession, I witnessed the ticker tape of my blood pressure dipping further. My pulse was over 120—very rapid. My puppet legs were being stuffed abruptly into pneumatic shock trousers.

I think this means I'm in the beginning stages of cardiovascular collapse.

"Can we hang another unit of packed RBCs?" a voice barked to my left. There was a distant response: "Call down for some fresh frozen plasma, too!" I felt the faint pressure of more items stacked on my abdomen.

Shapeless figures zipped in and out of my peripheral vision. Without glasses, I was lost in the blur of shadows. The external chaos didn't match how calm my body felt. No pain at all, just wilting at an exponential rate.

More clipboards and beeps. I forwent the hasty calculations on remaining blood volume as they wheeled the crash cart to the side of my bed. They thrust my gurney into a reclined position with my feet high in the air and my head near the floor. Trendelenburg position. I knew what that meant.

Darkness.

CHAPTER TWELVE

A STITCH IN TIME

A few hours later, I learned this was all because of one rowdy stitch that had unraveled. It forced the on-call surgeon to interrupt his turkey sewing in his kitchen to instead engage in human sewing in the operating room. Though my anatomical world was knit back together, I felt a perceptible wrinkle in my psyche. That crease from my NDE-lite altered every perspective and angle. Everything in my world seemed 'off' just one millimeter, like a pair of irregular jeans on the clearance rack. Or the sickly green cast on the sky before a tornado.

Several weeks later, I started my first day back at work. I drove my familiar commute along the snow-covered country roads. Previously refreshing, the cold winter sunrise now appeared bleak against the crunching of my tires on the gravel parking lot. I hoisted my tote onto my shoulder and shuffled to unlock the heavy clinic door. Was it always this difficult to open?

Once inside, the familiar warmth and soft sounds of morning conversation could be heard from the front office. Just how I liked it. I preferred showing up early, before the melee. I shrugged my coat off and put it on the rack. My Danskos clunked across the sterile linoleum to my office. The pale glow from my computer screen silhouetted the mound of paperwork waiting for me.

Deep breath. First days are hard. Even harder when there's been a shift in the universe.

I peeked at my homecoming schedule. To my delight, I had an easy arrangement of the typical potpourri of rural family medicine: sore throats, well-child visits, depression, diabetes, hypothyroidism. No doubt, this was the work of my dear nurse. I smiled, imagining her as the club bouncer, knocking people off my schedule in hopes I could have a slow return to normalcy.

My first patient was a sweet seventy-two-year-old grandma. Her shriveled hands clutched a handwritten list of top concerns, written neatly on yellowed paper featuring Garfield at the top. Worrying was her favorite pastime, and I wondered if her current troubles might also have originated in 1986, just like her memo pad. Thankfully, she accepted my redirection easily that day. I reframed most of her concerns with rapid-fire assurances in the ten minutes of allotted visit time.

"No, Gladys, I *promise* that rash is not syphilis."

"Yes, it's perfectly normal to have a few whiskers grow on your chin."

"I have no idea why your left earlobe has been tingling for the last forty years."

I adore little old ladies, sharp as they can be. Even those that dwindle into faded existence, bedridden and demented in their last years, share the same current of worry. Generalized anxiety is what keeps all women alive, like the 103-year-old woman who was wheeled into the exam room by her nursing home caregiver. A matriarch to dozens of great-grandchildren, she was a legacy, despite being unable to walk after years of dementia.

She slept upright during her whole physical exam. As I lifted the hem of her pants, I noticed turgid, swollen legs. Pink and firm, they felt nearly wooden. I asked the caregiver to have her lie down more often and elevate her legs to allow proper circulation.

"Oh, doc. I wish we could! We try to get her to lie down, but she refuses. She wants to sleep sitting up. She is convinced that if she lies down, she'll die," the caregiver replied with a curt nod.

"Ah, I see," I replied, typing this in her electronic medical records. I clicked the mouse and the woman sputtered to life.

Her heavy wrinkled lids lifted, exposing tired eyes. She turned her head to face me, surveying the surroundings.

"What...is...*that?*" she asked in her gravelly voice, looking at the computer keyboard.

"This is a *computer!*" I responded. I patted the monitor with my hand and repeated the word, "Com-pute-r!" I exaggerated my typing like Liberace at the piano and explained, "This is where I keep your medical information!"

She paused for one moment. "Fantastic. I'll *take it!*"

The caregiver and I chuckled as she wheeled her out with my recommendations to lie down for a few hours so her body could redistribute that swollen fluid. The next day, I received a call that she had passed away. To this day, I'm convinced this is why moms never lie down.

I opened the door of the next room and greeted my second patient of the day: a fifty-two-year-old male named John. We had had somewhat of a contentious relationship over the years. Often, it took months for him to accept any new diagnosis. Several times he'd walked out of the office with a precariously high blood pressure of 200/110, despite my urgent threats about risks of untreated hypertension (Stroke! Heart attack! Death!). He'd return the following week with headaches and fatigue as a result, only to leave again with a different excuse: "I'm sure it's just 'white coat syndrome.' I get nervous around you docs, and my pressure rises," he'd proclaim. Rinse and repeat.

John was the reason I regretted my summer jobs in college. Instead of working at Blockbuster video, I should've spent my summers patrolling my uncle's used car lot. If I could convince a reasonable, well-educated person that this rusty car could outlast the next decade of Midwest winters, I would be ready for the onslaught of the modern primary care patient. The latest Google search or personal blog gives patients infinite power to deny, accuse, or thwart your best intentions. It can be a verbal *Battle Royale* that lasts several rounds of office visits—until something finally yields or a worse crisis unfolds in the ER.

That day, in addition to John's existing high blood pressure, his blood work also showed a high sugar level. This predictability was baked right into the carbohydrate crust of modern American health. As people approach middle age, stress mounts, weight increases, blood pressure rises, glucose follows, and dementia is the icing on top.

I sank onto the stool from the lead weight of my white coat.

My wrists assumed their position over the computer keyboard. He confessed, "Look, Doc. I already know what this means. I got the 'sugar diabetes.' My grandma and uncles had it, too. But maybe I could just eat better?"

Years ago, this display of self-directed motivation might have inspired me to cheerlead this man to build new habits. Instead, I stared at the digital time on the computer screen. Eight minutes remained of John's fifteen-minute visit.

A deep sigh of responsibility escaped my lips.

Ever since I returned from my dose of NDE-lite, the reality of a modern career in family medicine was glaring. It appeared strikingly oppositional to what I had wanted. I hadn't even noticed the insidious crumbling of our influence over a patient's health. Our expertise and training had slowly been replaced with meaningless duties. It was obvious to me now that I was just a robotic data-entry technician fighting constant pop-up alert fatigue, trying to comply with the latest regulations before an office visit concluded.

I finished clicking the remaining boxes on my computer screen to complete the "quality measures" and tossed a civil nod in his direction. Then, I uncharacteristically slaughtered his enthusiasm with a bitter dose of post-NDE-lite reality:

"Listen, we both know that eating better won't make a difference, John. I can predict what will happen. You might eat healthier for a bit, and then you'll have a hard time keeping it up, and we'll be back here again in six months. Let's just start you on metformin 500 mg twice daily." I pressed "send" and immediately faxed it to the pharmacy. I pulled a generic handout titled

You and Diabetes and pushed it across the counter. "I'll see you back in three months."

I think he could feel the new wrinkle in my tapestry, too.

He left without a word.

CHAPTER THIRTEEN
PAUL RIDDY

"I'm sure you'll find your balance again soon!" a nurse chirps over my shoulder.

It had been weeks since my reintroduction back at work, and I still couldn't seem to find my bearings. "Balance" is a fairytale. It doesn't exist. It's a mythical fantasy word wrapped in a promise of control and precision.

That one-legged yoga tree pose might look effortless, but inside, my body was a bundle of trembling muscle fibers and blood coursing through my veins. Even in osteopathic medicine, there's an ephemeral term "Still point," named after the founder of osteopathy, Dr. A.T. Still. This is the moment when the perfect traction, support, and pull of tissues invites a harmonious relaxation of the body. It exists, but never for long.

Just when it feels that balance is attained, it's over. The very moment the last shirt was folded in my clean laundry pile, there was a new dirty sock added. Or the brief celebration of a fully stocked pantry and fridge before it was ravaged by teenagers. The earth keeps spinning and the universe continues its swirling chaos and preordained imbalance.

Nothing is more fictitious than work/life *balance*. And yet, I remember clinging to hope as a young working mother. I read every article and book about balance. I wanted to believe in something. I loved fairy tales. If this mythical work/life balance had an ambassador, it would be Paul Riddy.

"Paul Riddy. Paul Riddy. Paul Riddy." This was the mechanized sound that the breast pump murmured over and over behind my closed office door years prior.

"PaulRiddyPaulRiddyPaulRiddy..."

The day I carried an electronic milking machine into my office, I had triumphed. I was a walking representative of someone who does it all.

Every three hours, Paul Riddy's serene cadence tricked me into believing I had achieved perfect balance as a contemporary working woman, hero of work and hearth, balanced on point. All credit to Paul, he was masterfully suave at distraction. Once his song was over, the return to reality was jarring. Avalanches of paperwork reappeared with everything marked "urgent," reminding me that "balance" is indeed a fleeting illusion.

So when things don't seem right, what do humans do? We search for reason. Logic. Patterns. Anything to alleviate our feelings of powerlessness.

Maybe applying relational logic can help. When I was unsure how many miles we'd driven on the family road trip, I'd count the increase of vulgar Mad Lib word suggestions. Quantifiable relationships like these can help define current reality, similar to the classic 80/20 Pareto Principle: 20 percent of your efforts yield 80 percent of your results. Happens all the time in a medical career: 20 percent of a population consume 80 percent of our healthcare resources.

Searching for answers, I started reapplying this principle to my life:

> Twenty percent of the rooms in my home were where I spent 80 percent of my time.
> There were a zillion apps on my iPhone, but I only used 20 percent of them regularly.

Only 20 percent of my children's winter gloves would ever match each other.

I hadn't used this 80/20 rule since early medical school training. It was what saved my wobbly brain from embarrassment at 6 a.m. "What percentage of pemphigoid cases are *bullous*?" the attending barked. If my brain thought the answer was "a little," I would guess 20 percent; if it was "a lot," I'd say 80 percent.

"Eighty percent are bullous pemphigoid," I declared with faux Emmy-winning confidence.

"Correct," the attending replied.

It was easy to slip into this dynamic of numbers and metrics. While I might assume logic could solve almost any problem, I had forgotten that a significant part of healing was immeasurable. A medical career has roots in the sacred space of trust and partnership, built on a strong foundation of science. At its most fundamental core, a physician was a creative master—using all five senses to comprehend the condition of a patient. A half dozen diagnoses manifested after observing their slouched posture and downcast eyes (depression), palpating their dry skin texture (dehydration), listening to their prolonged raspy breaths (emphysema), and smelling their fruity breath (diabetes). Then, the physician weaved the patient's past history and present circumstances to spin a tapestry of their future. All within moments.

But there I was, slogging back into the routine of patients. And it felt so...industrial. Mechanized. Methodical. I couldn't pretend any longer that *this* was a healing space.

Open door. Sit down. Say hello. Wait eighteen seconds before interrupting. Look at screen. Type on keyboard. Click mouse. Look at screen. Look at patient. Stand up. Listen to heart. Listen to lungs. Sit down. Click mouse. Type on keyboard. Click mouse. Type. Click. Type. Click.

Was I even a doctor? Was *this* what a career in medicine had become? Was I even making a difference?

The pharmacist was right. An NDE-lite shifted my perspective, and I was feeling the long-lasting results. I saw that I was a drone, marching in and out of tiny rooms all day, carrying around my disembodied spirit. Something felt wrong. My installed robotic software was lagging and buffering. Rushing between exam rooms left no time to adjust. Must. Finish. Before. The. Mandatory. Noon. Meeting.

My frame was perched in front of another nondescript middle-aged person as he was describing his abdominal pain. My audio settings must have been off that day, as Mr. Thomas's words weren't registering.

My mind was still with the previous patient sitting in the adjacent room: Scott.

Scott was a freshman in college. I had known him for years, as his mother would bring him in for routine school physicals. He excelled in our small town's high school track team, earning top grades, and winning a scholarship to a coveted university.

It surprised me to see his name in my schedule. College students rarely needed medical care. But his mom noticed a significant change as he returned home for a weekend visit: He had lost weight and appeared despondent and melancholy.

When I had entered Scott's room moments before, I felt the cold air seep past my steel robotic casing. Apparently, my empathy wasn't completely defunct. As Scott candidly described his suicidal plan, I silently assembled the next steps in my head. He agreed to stay in the room while we made some phone calls to keep him safe and start his recovery.

"...it's like a dull ache that comes in sharp waves..." Mr. Thomas broke my fog as he droned on about his belly pain. Slowly, my audio dissolved into a cacophony of noise: the soft sobs from Scott in the next room. The murmur of conversation in the hallway. The bang of another exam room door closing. Heavy boots stepping onto the scale. Phones beeping on hold. Sterile pouches ripping open. Surgical steel clinking onto trays. Car doors slamming outside. Snow plows scraping the concrete.

And that's when I heard it.

A harsh buzzing noise.

Bzzzzzz.

Like a hornet trapped in a stiff envelope.

BZZZZZZTT.

CHAPTER FOURTEEN

A MOST SHAMEFUL CELEBRATION

BZZZZZZZT!!!!

My head tilted to the side as I located the sound. The buzzing belonged to the dispensing machine in the hallway, as it spit out labels for each new patient registration.

That day, the sound announced a plot twist in my life. Another chapter closed. Act one was done. I would never go back.

The sound was much more than "just another patient registration." The buzz represented the failure of my skills to reorganize my life. A harsh glaring siren of defeat. Over the last fifteen years—on paper—I'd tried all the methods to guarantee a work-life balance in the spreadsheet of a medical career. I worked longer hours, fit more patients into my schedule, shortened their office visits, improved my coding skills to capture better revenue, increased my typing speed, offered more in-office procedures—and yet, my joy decreased while my stress increased.

This was one logic puzzle that was unsolvable with numbers or determination.

I couldn't keep up with new variables in this equation: Google searches from patients that required more than a three-minute explanation. Press Ganey scores that could plummet if you didn't provide the requested narcotic medication or antibiotic. Doctors

were no longer valued as healers, instead viewed as robotic sup-
pliers in a factory line of 'medical care.'

BZZZZZT.

I concluded Mr. Thomas's visit and escorted Scott to his
mother's car so that she could drive him to our local psychiatry
floor. I retreated to my office bunker. Like a bell tolling my sur-
render, my body responded by deflating onto the exercise ball
that had become my office chair (yet another remnant of multi-
tasking attempt to tone my core while working).

My medical assistant appeared in the doorway and casually
dropped a newspaper obituary on my desk. Another beloved
patient, an eighty-five-year-old lady, had finally passed away
from a long battle with cancer. I noticed her face in the newspaper clipping, decades younger than when I last saw her for a
sprained ankle. She was a Midwest farmer, tough in every way.
Nothing would stop her, not even an ACE-wrapped ankle.

When cancer was diagnosed years prior, she met this challenge with equal parts of stoicism and practicality. She refused
to give cancer center stage. She continued to bring photos of her
grandchildren and garden vegetables to our office visits. She'd
boast with pride about winning top prizes in the state fair (for
her squash, not the grandchildren).

Normally, this obituary would prompt me to open my desk
drawer, pull out stationery, and script a short message to her
family, expressing gratitude for being a part of her life.

That day was different.

My desk drawer didn't open. My hands remained limp
on my lap.

Instead of remorse, a surge of happy relief surprised me.

One! Less! Patient!

I felt the corner of my mouth upturn at the idea. One less
patient. This meant one less phone call. One less message to
answer. One less medication to adjust. One less order to cosign.

One less person to squeeze into my booked schedule. One less prior authorization to submit. One less vaccination to peddle.

As soon as the elation crested, a crushing wave of shame seared my soul, plummeting me into the deep end of despair: What kind of doctor celebrates the *death* of a beloved patient?!

Suddenly, the world felt tight and constricted. Shrink-wrapped around my body. I was suffocating in guilt, yet raw and exposed. My black soul was rotting in front of everyone, and it desperately needed oxygen. I abandoned everything on my desk: the obituary, the stacks of papers, faxes, and unsigned orders. I needed to flee. I hastily wedged my arms into my bulky winter jacket and burst into the frigid winter blast, nostrils splintering with ice.

I ignored the footsteps crunching behind me in the snow. Frantically, I yanked my car door open and collapsed inside. Securely locked in my motorized igloo, my attempt to escape this contemptuous crime.

"Dr. Salyer! Dr. Salyer!" One of the faces of our nurses popped up at my window. In the dark of midwinter's dusk, she glowed like a ghost. She must have followed my dishonorable black-sooted footprints in the snow. I was certain she could hear my scandalous thoughts.

She persisted, "Dr. Salyer! Don't leave yet! There are a few more urgent lab results you need to attend to!"

We exchanged thirty seconds of conversation through chattering teeth as I supplied the information she needed to return into the warm clinic and complete her tasks.

Yet there she remained. She glanced at my gloved hands gripping the frosty steering wheel.

She stared at me. I stared straight ahead.

Surely she knew. I couldn't stop the side effects of NDE-lite coursing through my brain.

I broke the silence. "It's 5:15 p.m. on Leap Year Day, Feb 29."

"Yes?" Her quizzical face was framed by snowflakes whirling around.

"Mark my words: By next Leap Year, I won't be here. I will be doing something else."

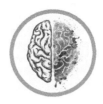

CHAPTER FIFTEEN

INTERNAL GPS, ACTIVATED

There are two kinds of people.

> There are olive lovers and olive haters.
> The coordinated and the clumsy.
> The huggers and those who prefer to shake hands.
> The napkin folders and napkin crumplers.
> Those with kids, and those who know how to raise them.

And then there are those of us who ask for directions, and the others that keep driving to see the exit ramp. I'm a direction-asker. Even worse, I'm a direction-asker with unrelenting road-trip anxiety. There must be an ICD-10 code for this. Before GPS and Siri, I relied on crumpled napkins with crooked maps scrawled on them. Uneasy with new roads, I'd routinely pull off the road *convinced* I already passed the exit. Countless numbers of blasé gas station attendants have steered me back on the road in exasperation.

This explains how I found myself in an unfamiliar office two weeks later. I needed some direction. I was tired of listening to myself whine, so I metaphorically pulled over to ask for directions.

This time, it wasn't a bored gas station attendant, but an EMDR therapist. EMDR, Eye Movement Desensitization and Reprocessing[2] was originally formulated as a treatment[3] to help with recovery from past traumatic events. Using right/left lateral stimulation and muscle activation while talking through the emotions allows the brain to communicate across the corpus callosum. Any simulation that alternatively activates the left and right side of your body and brain. These emotional (right brain) memories are given new meaning[4] as the logical side (left brain) processes them efficiently.

I was watching a horizontal light bar as the tiny red dots of light swept from left to right. Back and forth. This seemed so ridiculous, but I was willing to give anything a try.

She explained that any bilateral cross-body activity can produce similar benefits. That was how EMDR was discovered by Dr. Francine Shapiro. She noticed her uneasy feelings evaporated after her routine walks when she gazed alternatively to her left and right along her path. By stimulating right and left brain[5] cross-communication, it builds up neuroplasticity and resilience.

I desperately needed something.

I walked into her office expecting that EMDR could iron out that wrinkle in my psyche. Find the root of my NDE-lite and pluck it out. Mend my medical marriage to Hippocrates and allow me to return to my uninterrupted path as a rural family physician, mom of three.

Instead, I walked out with clarity and superhuman vision. I couldn't go back. This was a new beginning. A redo. A mulligan. An opportunity to re-evaluate and realize that I had changed and I no longer fit the system around me.

My heart broke under the realization of it all.

There was only one way forward. I wrote a letter to my first love: my medical career.

CHAPTER SIXTEEN
THE FATHER OF MODERN MEDICINE

Dear Hippocrates,

I respect your efforts as the father of modern medicine. Your influence is undeniable in founding this profession.

But a lot has changed since 350 B.C.

I want a divorce.

You and I were young, idealistic, and naive when we met. Everyone said we were perfect for each other: valedictorian and humanitarian. We thought we could change the world, one sacrifice at a time. Sleep deprivation, grueling academic hurdles, delayed gratification. We proudly wore those badges as a testament to our commitment together when we started our board-certified family medicine profession in 2003.

I fell in love with you from the very beginning without knowing the ending, but I barely tended to my own needs. To me, the sacrifice was worth it.

I should've signed a prenup.

Slowly, the tendrils of distrust curled around our world. You invited others into our relationship without my consent: insurers, attorneys, administrators, and then, Google.

Insurers didn't trust our decision-making, so formularies became a paradoxically rigid moving target. Patients wouldn't trust our recommendations, certain that their latest internet search was far more medically sound. Hospital administration stepped in to intervene. Before we knew it, our world became a time- and date-stamped arena, visible to all, helpful to none. Once a pillar of scientific benevolence, doctors were stripped of power and treated with public skepticism.

To rein in this metastatic distrust, you suggested we collect and curate data. Surely, this would "improve" our nation's floundering health-care system, right? Never mind the suicidal grandpa in room three, but did he agree to get his colonoscopy and tetanus updated? Who cares if the basal cell skin cancer was recognized and treated on Mrs. Haywood; did she sign up for a mammogram? My resentment grew with each step into this minefield of check boxes.

This wasn't the life I planned for us. The inequality felt oppressive. I gazed longingly at our neighbors: the specialists. Their grassy-green lives appeared unfettered by regulations because they could just divert any responsibility with one sentence, "Follow up with your primary care doctor."

But I couldn't.

Your expectations of our relationship had morphed into something unrecognizable. Gone were the moments I hoped to bask in the glow of empathy, caring, and healing. Do you recall the vows we took, Hippocrates? "I will remember that there is art to medicine as well as science, and that warmth, sympathy, and understanding may outweigh the surgeon's knife or the chemist's drug."

A far cry from your modern version. Today's words are icily brisk as we shiver past each other in the crowded hallways. You speak in modifiers, ICD-10 codes, and triplicate forms.

My love languages are touch and words. Yours is EMR. Your eyes practically glow brighter than the screen when a new data collection feature is unveiled, lengthening the nurse's duties from fifteen to twenty minutes for each patient check-in. It's obvious you love to flirt with inefficiency.

You shifted the boundaries of our relationship daily, expecting me to jump through unnecessary hoops against the backdrop of "more patient access." How can I detect the insidious hemochromatosis or educate the infertile polycystic patient when I'm interrupted with your ridiculous demands to answer every message or refill with neck-breaking speed?

First, do no harm, correct?

Yet, I continued to adapt my workflow to be more efficient, clinging to the knowledge that if I didn't care, who would? I worked harder; you paid me less. And now all we do is fight over money when we should fight over our real downfall: your adultery. When you stepped out and had an affair with Press Ganey, you changed the tapestry of our relationship forever.

In your short-sighted effort to measure value based on antiquated patient satisfaction scores, you placed my vitality and compassion in hospice. How can my worth be stripped down to a number when I'm pressured to see more volume, squeezing as much as I can into fifteen minutes? I feel underappreciated, and I deserve better.

It's not about the money, Hippocrates. It never was. No matter how many miles I run, sun salutations I cycle through, or glasses of wine I sip, I have still come to the conclusion that our core values have become incompatible.

Irreconcilable differences.

In closing, I am not angry; I'm disappointed. I'm filled more with gratitude for our time together. Relationships aren't measured in length, but the quality of growth and meaning. Because of you, I have an amazing skill set, memories to fill my heart, and a clear foundation to pursue my next relationship, customizable to my definitions.

Best wishes,

Your American family doctor

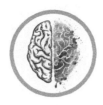

CHAPTER SEVENTEEN
SECOND PUBERTY

If there is such a thing as Second Puberty, I was living it. I was undergoing some kind of existential metamorphosis as a result of this new NDE insight.

I was trying to read. Even with earplugs lodged deep into my ears, I could still hear it.

Nothing could pull my attention away from that sound. Not the whine of our dog pawing for a chew toy under our couch. Not the blaring performance of Rihanna's latest hit from Emery's bedroom.

Even the sound of Owen bounding up our basement steps and sporting a new "man bun" atop his head went unnoticed.

I clenched my teeth and continued focusing on the sentence in front of me.

CJ emptied the trash, shaking the garbage bag with such violent and unnecessary vigor, I felt a scream curdle in my throat. And yet, even this didn't outdo the noise that captivated all my attention.

It was the sound of supersonic chewing broadcasted from the mandibles of our youngest, Beckett.

Trying to reinvent oneself in Second Puberty was difficult.

I became as irritable and determinedly independent as any teen. I was a bitter blend of indignant tones with a dollop of anxiety. If I was on the Starbucks menu, I would have been

"Iced Conviction with a Double Shot of Doubt." I challenged any person that dared to suggest physicians should just "be more resilient."

Trapped in my highly sensitive body, my mind ping-ponged around my skull without direction. Searching for purpose, I became a lit neon sign, open 24/7 to every idea that floated by.

I knew something had to change, but I had no idea how. So I started searching for the CliffsNotes for this next semester.

A few weeks later, I found myself with other doctors in a semi-pubertal transition, on the brink of blossoming self-discovery. We all signed up for a conference titled "Physician Wellness." It was a pseudo-John-Hughes-Breakfast-Club Saturday cloistered together in a stale conference room. Complete with a full cast of characters: the jaded semi-retirees, calloused Gen X-ers, fresh-faced new graduates, perfectionistic moms, angry futurists…and me: highly sensitive and nowhere to turn.

There we were, sipping water and awkwardly doodling on notebooks. Just like high school. Except, instead of a class about "How Your Body Will Change," today's topic was "Burnout." The moderator was a calm, caring doctor with a pleasantly neutralizing presence. Like human Alka-Seltzer for your psyche. She smoothed the turbulent burn of our collective angst, and before long, we sat closer. We volunteered our vulnerable stories of fractured lives and uncertain futures.

This was an identity audit of sorts. Our existence had unconsciously become a series of maligned adaptations as we slowly molded behaviors to fit habitual patterns expected of us. Just like side-stepping over that creaky spot in the hallway, even though our "baby" was now fifteen years old and didn't nap. Likewise, physicians are groomed to accept whatever lands on our desks, in our schedules, and on our minds without training or support to sift through our own existential mess. We collect praise for sleepless nights, last-minute saves, and taking on superhuman responsibility.

The identity of "doctor" had molded our lives to sustain its presence. We shared our stories, reflecting on our own attempts to conform. Yet no amount of speed typing or efficient templates in our electronic medical records could help. As much as we wanted a paperless world, our desks carried the burden of cascading faxes, nursing home reports, prior authorizations, referral letters, and memos. We adapted in our own ways. Some requested Fridays off. Some signed up for Zumba. Some took luxurious vacations every few months. Some grew cancer. Some signed divorce papers. Some drank too much. Some thought about swallowing that handful of pills.

Those of us who carry the double X chromosome on top of the "doctor" label felt heavy with our supplemental responsibilities. Our office chair never grew cold. It often supported an endless line of tearful nurses seeking solace after the male doctor had *another* one of his paper-throwing tantrums. Our schedules seemed to overflow with patients seeking help for complicated emotional topics like *depression, low libido,* and *trauma* because we're "easier" to talk to. Our eye muscles were toned and fit as we learned to suppress eye rolls as people asked how our "maternity *vacation*" went.

Similar to the introductions from the first day of medical school, we listened to the identities of our fellow comrades: father, pilot, grandmother, butterfly collector. I contemplated what was stamped on my imaginary identity card.

By the end of our conference, we understood that we shared the same labels with over half of practicing physicians in America: low perceived personal achievement, disempowerment, and emotional exhaustion.

We walked out with a fresh identity stamp on our cards: *burned out.*

CHAPTER EIGHTEEN
SECRETS

Just because a new label has been uncovered doesn't mean it was ready for public display. I purposefully hid my *burnout* label out of sight, tucked away like a secret. Not unlike those tattered and worn ornaments on our family Christmas tree. No one throws away an ornament; it is an important historical artifact. No matter how broken or awkward, they deserve a spot.

However, no one wants to be greeted by a ceramic vision of Santa sitting on a chimney toilet, either. This is the unspoken truth of all mothers everywhere: we rearrange the ornaments after the kids go to bed. Someone's got to keep the holiday peace (and symmetry). Placing the unsightly ones in the back, we showcase our sparkliest ornaments in the front.

Aren't we all walking virtual Christmas trees? We highlight our envious images on Instagram (with the appropriate vivid Juno filter), but leave the tattered and stained yoga pants out of frame. Just as Rumi says, "You are the entire ocean in a drop." We contain everything from ugly to beautiful. I just wasn't ready to find a branch to hang my burnout memento quite yet. It was too fragile and risky.

The next day in my office, I secretly began my mission to find purpose once again. I tilted my computer screen away from the bustle of staff in the doorway. I opened Google and typed in "second careers for physicians." Suggestions popped up: expert witness training, depositions, prison healthcare, medical writing...and cake decorating.

I tried on scenarios in my mind:

Velvety fondant under my fingers in a small cafe, sunlight peering in the window. The smell of lemons and raspberries.

Or...the thick atmosphere of high-pressure courtrooms, surrounded by shoulder pads and clicky pens.

Metal detectors and prison cells.

Nope. Not for me.

I continued my search. Medical writer. Hospital administration. Malpractice expert.

Nothing was appealing. Dread creeped in. Now what? What happens when your new label fits so well and requires you to adjust everything else in your life? When do you quit? When do you keep going?

How do you know when *enough is enough?*

This question has plagued centuries of humanity—in their marriages, education, careers, chemotherapy, sculpting, writing, war. When is *enough?*

The Zen proverb would tell us, "Let go, or be dragged."

The last time I was dragged, I was four years old. I was clutching the shaggy chestnut fur of my grandpa's dog as I rode him around the funeral home. Aptly nicknamed "Horse," I loved that dog. I'd crouch forward, like a mini-jockey, and we'd weave in and out of funeral wreaths, chasing bank robbers into the forest and finding jewels in abandoned castles. All before my mom finished clipping the last nose hair on the corpse of the moment.

I rewarded Horse with leftover sandwich crusts, which he'd catch in midair with his happy, slobbery mouth. When there was a lull in adventure, we'd find a shady spot under a big oak and I'd rest my head on his pillow of fur.

Until one day, I arrived with Mom for another routine day of mortal makeovers. (With all the makeover shows on prime time, how has *this* not aired?!) Horse didn't greet us at the door. Grandpa gave no explanation of his absence; it was business as usual. Phones still rang. The hearse needed gasoline. Coffins needed polishing. I suppose when you're around death every day, it becomes a routine part of life.

Even as a preschooler, I could sense that Horse's death held a trace of secrecy. Family members spoke in hushed tones. I grieved the only way I knew how. I gathered as many flowers and weeds as I could hold in my tiny arms and arranged them around the fresh mound of earth in the ravine where he was buried. Horse deserved a regal funeral.

It wasn't until decades later that I learned the truth.

That morning, a phone call interrupted my grandpa from the embalming process. He left the room temporarily, and when he returned, he noticed something so horrific and taboo, he refused to tell the story for decades. It was shameful. Negligent. And the worst thing that could befall a man. Dead or alive.

Grandpa returned to notice a crucial pair of anatomical items were missing from the groin. Horse was found later that evening, stiff from his formaldehyde-filled nutty snack. No one was told about this egregious act. It lived on as a dark, untold crime in our family.

"Everyone has secrets," my mom justified.

"Be careful. You are what you eat," my dad chuckled.

That was about the only nutrition advice I was taught as a child. You are what you eat. In my youth, that meant I was 10 percent orange Kool-Aid, 30 percent Hostess snacks, and 60 percent Midwest meat and potatoes.

Food can be so many things: a love language, a distraction, a security blanket. For my childhood family, it was an afterthought. When my next Google search stumbled across a five-day medical conference that promised organic meals, yoga, and stress relief, I was curious. If I was what I ate, maybe I could reinvent myself.

At that time, I had one foot out the door of my career already. I needed to redeem my remaining Continuing Medical Education (CME) credits before jumping ship on this family medicine career. Might as well spend it in Austin, Texas, to see what the Institute of Functional Medicine was all about.

Weeks later, I packed my apathy and uncertainty into my carry-on bag. The last thing on my mind was learning *more* medicine. Truthfully, I needed a break from life, motherhood, and existential angst.

Now I understand how unsettling Dorothy felt after landing in Oz. Entering this world of bright-eyed, fresh-faced, functional medicine professionals was blinding. This couldn't be real, I thought. Rich with academic research, each IFM lecture ended too soon for my craving. I couldn't get enough of the evidence-based findings on using vitamins, nutraceuticals, and nutrition prescriptions to heal chronic disease. How had this been around for twenty years and I was just learning of Dr. Jeffrey Bland, the founder of functional medicine, *now?* Conversations brimmed with topics on 'gut healing' and 'energy optimization,' things I had never heard in conventional medicine. I listened with rapt attention to colleagues describing their private practices with extra-long patient appointments. I felt a stirring in my soul.

After one of the lectures concluded with current research on fueling mitochondria with nutrition, I stepped away because I had another secret mission in Austin.

I was meeting someone important there. I found her online during my post-NDE dark days of soul searching on Google. This was the final ingredient to my juicy Lifetime movie plot: frustrating midlife crisis relieved with incognito online searching and a sprinkle of new relationships. I had been confiding in her for a few weeks already, and I couldn't wait to meet her.

My physician coach.

Like all high achievers, I immediately bristled at the word "coach." I didn't need *help*. I'd been doing life without a *coach* for nearly four decades. However, like the Physician Wellness conference months prior, this would become one of the most critical watershed moments of my life, paving the way for my humility as I learned from future mentors. Research shows that rates of reported burnout can decrease by 17 percent[6] after five months with a physician coach. After several sessions with her, I polished my awareness around boundaries, core values, and behavior change[7]. I understood how to reconnect with my autonomy and to choose my next steps[8].

More than just my coach, she was a marriage counselor, helping me fall back in love with medicine. After a few sessions, I realized I didn't want to leave the world of the healing arts. What I needed to do was bring the arts back into my personal delivery of medical care. I needed to practice medicine on my own terms with creativity and love.

CHAPTER NINETEEN

HOPE HAS NO DRESS CODE

Monday morning rolled around, and the family practice factory line rumbled alive again.

But that day was different.

I placed my stethoscope on little Annie's belly and dramatically cocked my head to the side and scrunched my face into a mask of intense concentration. She was in for her grade-school physical. "I can hear your breakfast in there!" I proclaimed.

She squealed with glee and her eyes widened.

"*Yes*! It's quite obviously the sound of milk...and cereal!" I peeked from the corner of my eye to see if my guess was correct (it usually was—80 percent of the time). Annie clapped her hands wildly.

That day, I was Dr. Pollyanna. Bright and cheerful because I had a new plan. I could reinvent *true* medicine right *here*. I had witnessed it with my own eyes: doctors that were enthusiastic with their patients because they were not prescribing Band-Aids to cover a *symptom*; they taught functional medicine *solutions*. They exchanged their mandated checklists with ingenious inspiration. Traded their lackluster burnout for creative bliss. Functional medicine reminded me why I chose a career in medicine: to impart health by educating patients.

I sat in front of Betty. Next to her was "Walter" (the name of her walker).

"Now that your pain is interfering with sleep, will you consider a low-dose anti-inflammatory medication?" I probed gently.

Betty replied in the same manner as all my independent widows, "Doc, I'm too scared of getting hooked on those pain pills."

Instead, Betty would limp from pain, risking daily hip fractures to proudly hoist her heavy grocery bags all by herself. Conventional wisdom recommended judicious use of an anti-inflammatory to keep a patient active and mobile. Unfortunately, this was not without risk. It was only a matter of time before that prescription would erode the stomach lining and cause a bleeding gastric ulcer.

Inspired to try something new, I started by applying basic functional principles to her recommendations. I suggested she avoid the top inflammatory foods (dairy, gluten, and sugar), as they can irritate ongoing pain. I fortified her gut lining with probiotics and extra vitamin D.

Several weeks later, Betty called back to report, "I can't believe it. I have been sleeping through the night, and my bones don't ache as much in the morning. I walked six blocks yesterday!"

A glimmer of hope sparked in my soul. Maybe I could make this work. Patients were craving this kind of care, and equally so, I craved feeling like a real doctor again. The true definition of doctor is *docere*, Latin "to teach." And I was educating patients on holistic ways to take care of their body, fulfilling my doctor role.

Though my outlook was sparkly and new, I continued to embrace a well-worn habit: my noon run. I floated over the sidewalk as my mind combed through ideas inspired from the IFM conference. The numbers added up: the IFM website tracked over a million requests per year for a functional provider by ZIP Code. Cleveland Clinic had a functional medicine department. Why couldn't our rural hospital use this kind of comprehensive care with shared group medical visits, supportive health coaching, and holistic solutions to help lower prescription copays?

Turning the final corner of my run, I crafted my ideal functional medicine department in my mind. It would contain no trace of typical sterile, cold hospital rooms. This clinic would embody lush vitality by inviting all senses to participate in this healing environment. I'd hang colorful art. Leafy greenery would reflect our innate connection with nature. Soft, plush couches to support collaboration and sharing. Fragrant aromas of earthy essential oils like clove, orange, and ginger, to ground and calm our nervous system. Warm beams of sunlight from east-facing windows.

I bounced back to my office and prepared for another afternoon of saving the world. Then I opened an email from the hospital administration.

MEMO TO ALL EMPLOYEES: Current wall decorations must be removed by the end of the month and replaced by framed prints with colors to match hospital branding.

NEW ANNOUNCEMENT: The clinic is now offering convenient virtual e-visits for minor complaints. These reports are located in a new folder. You are responsible for checking this in addition to messages, refills, cosigns, lab results, expiring orders, and telephone encounters. Response time is three hours.

LAB ANNOUNCEMENT: New lab results will be automatically released after thirty-six hours to the patient without explanation. Be prepared for collective panic, as patients have the ability to flood your inbox with messages as they worry why their sodium is marked in red at 134 instead of normal at 136.

Okay, that last sentence may have been my interpretation. I continued reading.

MANDATORY DRESS CODE REMINDER: All clinic employees must wear clothing that aligns with our mission and is appropriate to professionalism. Leggings are prohibited along with skirts and knee-high boots.

I glanced down and realized I was wearing the outlawed trifecta: skirt, leggings, and boots.

In a blink, I was transported back in time. I was a nervous third-year medical student again. Worried about fitting into the social norms of the complex ecosystem of an operating room. I just wanted to subsist, unnoticed and unharmed, to finish that month's rotation in gynecologic oncology surgery. The operating room was a land bustling with the traffic of nurses, surgical technicians, anesthesiologists, and equipment. The hot lights were searing the back of my exposed neck. The prominent surgeon stood to my left, and I could feel the otherworldly glow of his legendary surgical skills emanating from his statuesque frame.

It was the third hour of a deep pelvic surgery to remove ovaries and scar tissue from cancer. I just spent the last three hours with two cumbersome stainless steel retractors in my hands. I was a human tool. My only purpose was to provide the doctor and senior residents with enough visualization of the organs buried into the body cavity.

Three hours in, and my blueberry muffin had long been digested. My glucose level dipped precariously. My bladder was full and quivering. My feeble hands began cramping and my arm muscles trembled as I tried to steady the retractors' position. I was summoning all accessory muscles to my aid: I subtly shifted my weight to keep my legs from falling asleep; I breathed slowly in and out of my nose. When suddenly, the mighty surgeon barked his commands, "Scalpel! Cautery! Here. No. I said *HERE!*"

Flashes of steel glinted under the burning lights as the nurses supplied his open palms with instant utensils and sponges. My lower body, now wooden pegs, supported my contorted spine as I hunched over, grasping the retractors. I had a searing itch under my mask. I pursed my mouth in response.

The surgeon growled, "STUDENT! Pay *attention!*" I jolted upright, leaned in further, and feigned interest in the shadowy depths of a pelvic surgery I could not see.

And then:"STUDENT! Out of the way! You're *in the field.*" I leaned away, maintaining proper outward retraction with my stiff, marionette arms, and my body decaying under the warming lights like a stale carnival hot dog. "Student, are you *watching? Do you see this?!* Pay attention."

Back and forth. In and out. Too near, too far. Like Grover on *Sesame Street.*

That experience taught me one thing: There is no middle ground. Eventually, decisions must be made.

He repeated, "Are you *in* the field or *out?*"

I replied without hesitation, "I'm out, sir."

I knew then that surgery was not the specialty for me. I recognized that I didn't fit. That landscape might have been thrilling for some, but it was not my future. I was out. I required a life with bathroom breaks and the ability to scratch my nose at liberty.

Decades later, I experienced that same feeling. I had another itch that I couldn't scratch. I felt a hint of it on that wintery Leap Year Day when I told my nurse I'd be doing something different. Now I knew exactly what the itch meant: I wanted to create a new world of functional medicine.

But I couldn't scratch that itch in this environment.

I sat there, reading between the lines of this mandatory email, and the voice of the obstetrical surgeon haunted me once more: "Hey, are you *in* or *out?*"

I'm definitely out.

CHAPTER TWENTY

LEAP AND THE NET APPEARS

That Leap Year proclamation spoiled on my tongue each passing day. During that brief parking lot encounter, I predicted I'd be gone in four years. But four years was a long time to endure. Each day behind the factory line of family medicine felt excruciating when my heart had already moved on. How many more of these memos could I endure?

No wonder the prize for "Principal for a Day" gathered so many donations in my kid's grade-school fundraiser. We all yearn for autonomy. "You're not the boss of me!" is shouted in youth but softens to a whisper as we clock in to our corporate jobs.

"If I were principal, I would totally change what we do during Spirit Week," Owen remarked. "I'd make Monday 'Swear Day.' You could say anything you want and never get in trouble."

Freedom of expression.

The next day, I sat in front of my office computer, celebrating my own Swear Day silently in my mind with colorful explosions.

My logical left brain disregarded debate rules and launched its position first: *What the fuck are you thinking? Walk away from a stable career? Totally idiotic financial decision. You've wanted this since fifth grade. Can't you just tow the line for another twenty years in rural medicine? Just don't try so hard. Check the boxes, nod your head, and sit your Pollyanna ass down. If you leave now, what's on the other side? Do you really want all that other hassle of owning a business? Every job has its awful parts. It's deciding which 'shit sandwich' you would rather eat. What if this next sandwich is* worse?

My imaginative right brain glimmered with naive hope: *What if you spent the next twenty years* not *feeling apathetic? What if you didn't have to rush back from unpaid vacations to stacks of insurance paperwork? What if you tried on this entrepreneurial technicolor dream coat and it fit? What if life could be* better *than ever! What if every week was Spirit Week?*

A groan escaped my lips. The pit in my stomach grew wider as I stood on the edge of decision.

Until recently, I was following the script that a medical career would require certain ingredients: half a dozen staff, large hospital administration, larger patient panel, short medical visits. I was in a self-imposed cage with the door wide open.

It's more comfortable to think the earth flat, and the moon a mirage. Those might think space travel is unachievable and impossible. Astronaut living isn't for everyone. There is always a choice. Even inactivity is a choice.

I felt a glow emanate brighter at the thought of designing a new era in my career timeline. I wanted to be certified with the Institute of Functional Medicine to craft my own innovative medical clinic. I wanted to be the teacher I always yearned to be. I wanted to make my own Spirit Week, month, year, and decade so I could wear whatever the fuck I wanted.

Right brain's love of fashion ultimately won.

I resigned.

CHAPTER TWENTY-ONE

IT'S NOT YOU. IT'S ME.

"I'm leaving my job."

I looked into my dear husband's eyes with a new seriousness. I stared into those bright hazel depths that sparked with mischief when we first met. They appeared older and wiser after decades of a medical career. They knew the struggle.

This felt like betrayal.

Family medicine was woven right into the tapestry of our relationship. Our shared love of primary care preceded our first date. We studied for exams together. We answered each other's pager if the other was changing a diaper. Our wedding anniversary celebrations were way past silk or lace or cotton. We commemorated early bedtimes, CPAPs, and bite splints.

Our Midwest upbringing came with factory-installed passivity and casseroles. Even as far as we've come, radical honesty is utterly terrifying. Emotional transparency can feel either exhilarating or isolating.

I studied his gaze for a reaction. Would it be fear? Jealousy? Admiration? He stared back. His blank face reflected the soberness of my decision. I was straddling a fault line in our geological history together.

Then I hugged him.

In typical fashion, I couldn't contain my word incontinence. I narrated a lofty goal without concrete numbers. I spoke with emotions, not logic. But he knew by the second sentence out of my mouth that I was smitten with space travel. He knew there was no going back when I had already buckled my seat belt. He understood.

Right after he voiced his support, but before I could change my mind, I notified the hospital administration of my decision to resign by the end of the calendar year.

Transitions are awkward. Your voice cracks in puberty. Your glassware gets broken in the moving boxes. Space shuttles break through the atmosphere with turbulence. This was no different. The remaining months in employed family medicine were an uncomfortable mix of excited tension. By day, I was mollifying tiny breakups with my patients: "It's not you. It's me." By night, I was browsing the streets of our small town, searching for vacant office spaces.

Others' reactions only added to the unpredictability. Patients that had received my extraordinary effort over the years (every refill was last minute, every medication required hours on the phone to get insurance approval) were diffident and unblinking. And others that barely needed a routine physical were disproportionately grief stricken with tears and Kleenex. Likewise, hospital administration responded in their erratic ways: from supportive to punitive. All the while, my resolve remained impervious. Within months of my decision, I left my 'forever job' I thought I'd have for the rest of my days and walked out the door...

...and right through a different one. I turned the key to open my empty office space on our small town's historic square. The ancient door slammed behind me. I shuffled over to the center of the dusty floor and slumped down, sitting cross-legged in the vacancy.

What the hell did I just do? Must be the first official Swear Day of Spirit Week.

My thoughts raced. Each worry lofted high into the void, ricocheted off the stark white walls, and landed back onto my furrowed brow. The thrill of "creating a world I wanted to live in" abruptly felt ominous and heavy. The cosmos was crashing down as I felt the enormousness of doing *everything* by myself.

What the fucking hell have I done?

I may have swapped the "burnout" shit sandwich for a new, unfamiliar flavor. I traced the grooves etched in the chalky wood floor with my fingertip. What secrets were locked within this floor? Could I absorb the astute tips from those businesses that inhabited this space since 1872? I was humbly willing to learn from any bakery, cheese store, or vape shop.

The only way to pacify this anxiety was a tactic borrowed from the overwhelming med school days: make a list. If I organized my worries into categories, my angst would dwindle. Still seated on the empty floor, I yanked open my bag, grabbed a notebook, and started scribbling. I filled four pages with scrawl before pausing to look up.

I surveyed the room with new eyes. Now purged of my apprehension, the space no longer felt empty, but rather blank. Simple and pure. The four walls were suddenly canvases brimming with possibility and begging for paint.

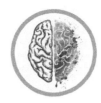

CHAPTER TWENTY-TWO

CODDIWOMPLING WE GO

"Yeah, but are you still a *real* doctor, though?" Beckett chirped in the passenger seat. It had been months since leaving my previous employment, and I was in the throes of arranging my private practice.

"Of *course* I'm *still a doc-tor*." I mustered my most convincing patience.

"But…you aren't even seeing patients," he pointed out.

Ouch.

I looked into the rearview mirror and met his gaze. It was a blameless question, not his fault. Kids are born with divining rods for our tender spots. I inhaled deeply before responding in my calmest voice: "When you go to school, aren't you still my son? And I'm still your mother, right?"

Beckett nodded in solemn agreement.

Kids are brilliantly intuitive. Like a peacock, they display our own neuroses with radiant fashion so we can have a second chance at rethinking our worldview. In the aftermath of his innocence, I realized how attached I was to my identity as a *physician*, a working woman who contributed equally to the monetary growth of my family.

That was something I learned about identity. It's always shifting, evolving. We are many things, and we are nothing. We are all things. How many labels do we assume? And how many do we achieve over our lifetime?

That evening, we were on our way to the grade-school spring concert, both too exhausted to partake in deeper conversation. We had just finished another high-intensity interval training session of motherhood: Dressing Up Your Grade Schooler. This timed event required dashing through a minimum of six rooms to locate matching shoes and the least-wrinkled shirt. The judges assumed a mother's skills would improve with each child, but agility wanes with age. Therefore, pacing is critically important. Start too strong, and both mother and child will quickly melt into a puddle of tears. Apply subpar effort, and it will be your child wearing their older sibling's stained khakis and a dayglo swim shirt onstage.

I entered the gymnasium to find a sea of heads. Spring concerts are the Lollapalooza of parenthood, but without sufficient mind-altering substances. Everyone who's anyone is there: parents, siblings, cousins, grandparents, babysitters, state senators. Like a drowning castaway, CJ's flailing arms signaled my attention, and I scooted into the empty seat he had risked life and limb to guard. Before I could ask if those were fresh claw marks on his forearms, the house lights dimmed. Together we sat silently for the next hour, watching kids tug at their hemlines under the sweltering stage lights.

Without warning, my anxiety jumped on center stage: *Am I still a doctor even if I don't sew up a laceration or do a pap smear? Am I a physician if I don't take insurance and opt out of Medicaid/Medicare instead?*

Children were herded on and off stage, teachers ushering them like loving shepherds. Finally, the oldest students began their song and a brave girl walked into the spotlight for her solo. She was wearing a flowery taffeta dress. Her white Mary Janes reflected the blinding spotlight, sending S.O.S. signals as she shuffled her feet nervously. The piano began, and she swallowed.

Her eyebrows knitted with trepidation as she opened her mouth toward the microphone perched in front of her.

At that moment, anything could happen. Her story was unwritten, and she was in full command of the pen. Would this mark an embarrassing and fleeting moment in her childhood history? Or would this be a proud milestone of creative independence? I started a silent pep talk in my head:

I know how you feel, O flowery young soloist. I am you. Yes, you're courageous under those hot lights. But I know you feel all our eyes are on you, waiting for your next moment. For the first time, my future is also 100 percent uncertain and 100 percent my own. It's scary, right? Maybe you didn't sleep well last night, either. Sometimes I jolt awake at 3 a.m., too. It's a spicy neurochemical cocktail of terror, shot right from my adrenals. (Don't worry, you don't need to know what that is for next week's science test.)

Wandering with uncertainty is scary. Old English slang had a word for this: "coddiwomple," meaning to travel purposefully toward an as-yet-unknown destination. Maybe that will be a new vocabulary word next week. Take note, flowery girl. You can do this.

Her voice began. A single trembling note, broadcasted into the atmosphere. Her fists clenched briefly at her sides. She continued her aria, her pitch wavering…coddiwompling perhaps.

You got this, flowery girl. Keep going. Your voice will find its stability. I 'coddiwompled' during my first night on call as a new intern doctor, too.

I was entrusted with an entire hospital floor with no knowledge of what would happen. It was the most frightening *Choose Your Own Adventure* book ever published. When you're on call, you're given a belt of pagers and a small windowless room in the basement of the hospital to hide. I remember lying on that stiff mattress, just waiting in complete terror for the shrill siren of a pager. Never knowing if it would signal a cardiac arrest or a simple signature request. A pager is the teeniest piece of intimidating plastic ever invented.

When the pager squealed for the first time, gastric acid burned my throat and I nearly burped my heart onto the scratchy bedsheets.

I dialed the number, and a tired nurse started her monologue, "Hi, um, *Doctor*"—throat clearing—"I have a thirty-two-year-old male here, post-op from uncomplicated appendectomy, complaining of a headache. No fever, surgical incision looks fine. Just wondering if I could give him some Tylenol?"

My brain stuttered. I glanced at the tiny television screen in the on-call room. CNN was running a segment on the dangers of fireworks. It was July 1st, the witching hour when all hospitals invite a fresh batch of newbie interns, and *this* was my first quest as a 'doctor'? A few moments later, I croaked, "Uh, yeah... sure, I guess?"

The nurse responded, "What dose, please?"

Wait. There was a *dose* on *Tylenol*? What was the generic name? My first quest as a new doctor and it was regarding an over-the-counter medication that I couldn't recall.

CNN's anchor was wearing an ill-fitting helmet and cumbersome flak vest while demonstrating various explosives. My brain was combusting in synchrony.

Thankfully, my brain eventually thawed, and I remembered the dose (325 mg). The patient did fine.

And for other issues, those hard-working nurses were there to help ease that abrupt transition from medical student to doctor.

Flowery girl's voice had started the third refrain. Her face transformed before our eyes. A smile flickered at the edge of her mouth. Her wobbly tone now replaced by a melody floating in the air with growing confidence as she was now supported by a choir of voices.

You're doing it, girl! Getting outside our comfort zones is hard, but so rewarding. Just like those nurses helped me long ago, your classmates are supporting you. I promise all the best things come on the other side of bravery.

Flowery girl was blooming in all her magnificence. Her cheeks, flushed from the lights, were full and plump from her gleaming smile. She pierced the auditorium with the last stanza, delivered with such strength and clarity. The final sweet note hung for a moment in the air.

Until the roar of a standing ovation.

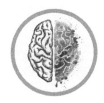

CHAPTER TWENTY-THREE

NEAR-DEATH EXPERIENCE MEETS NEW RELATIONSHIP ENERGY

As young doctors are released into the wild, their brains are so weak from training, they don't have the energy to discern which job might fit them best. Like Hallmark cards announcing the next level of their relationship, they sift through picturesque brochures overflowing from their mailboxes. Every glossy advertisement announces "*exciting* employment opportunities" or promises a "thriving medical practice in an *ideal* setting" with "a generous sign-on bonus" and only "minutes away from a cultural mecca!" Stock photos feature charming mountains, bustling city centers, and indistinguishable families dipping their toes in a serene lake. Airbrushed doctors smile in crisp white coats as they stand in solidarity within a sleek, modern hospital hallway.

Desperate to make a dent in their half-million dollars of medical school debt, most of them willingly trade their autonomy for any stable salary. They sign on so quickly, they don't even notice the invisible handcuffs of a floundering medical system.

If brochures were truthful, they would display unfiltered photos of pajama-clad doctors finishing charts at 10 p.m. while their spouse is tucking the kids in bed. They would show the kids bickering in the back seat of a stuffed minivan as the doctor drives over two hours to the "cultural mecca." Disillusioned doctors with Stockholm syndrome would be slumped over in mandatory meetings, wearing masks of resignation.

There I was, metaphorically holding a blank brochure in my hand. I could design my new medical career however I wanted. With notecards at my side and highlighters in my palm, I deepened my infatuation with functional medicine. Like a lovestruck schoolgirl, I couldn't stop thinking about my new crush. I was blissful in my New Relationship Energy (NRE), and I used that passion as the architect to create my new world.

I immersed myself in a heady cloud of obsession. I doodled intricate biochemical pathways on my notebooks like a dreamy teen would write her crush's name on the back of her geometry folder. Instead of a romantic soundtrack, my playlist featured podcasts like *Evolution of Medicine's Functional Forum* and Alex Charfen's *Entrepreneurial Personality Type*. Evidence of my love wasn't measured in wilted roses or empty chocolate boxes, but recycling bins overflowing with discarded toxins, like BPA plastics and lotions with phthalates and parabens. My lashless eyes were opened to our toxic world, and I wanted nothing other than the warm embrace of holistic medicine.

Unfortunately, my new love had some serious competition: imposter syndrome. Since life is littered with moments of doubt, if we're not careful, imposter syndrome will link arms and stumble with us like a drunk partygoer whose ears are deaf to the word "enough." It delights in this persistent internalized fear of being exposed as a 'fraud' and leaves its evidence all around. Imposter syndrome is visible in dried coffee stains from late nights in the office, completing projects that stop nothing short of *perfect*. It is recognized on the bank receipts for more trainings and conferences to quell the insecurities.

As a perfectionistic, high-achieving Sagittarius, imposter syndrome is directly encoded in my genes. I'm certain I have extra SNPs (single nucleotide polymorphisms) for "Too Good

To Be True" and "Are You Sure You Know What You're Doing?" Imposter syndrome haunted me during early motherhood and reappeared as the most dangerous rival of entrepreneurism.

Those nasty hardwired thinking patterns can be difficult to eradicate. If I found myself questioning my audacity to run a medical business and felt my heart start palpitating, I'd immediately stop. And I'd do what I was trained to do in any crisis: the ABCs of cardiopulmonary resuscitation.

Airway. I'd unclench my jaw and peel my tongue from the roof of my mouth. I'd part my mouth and let my face relax. Roll my neck in circles and feel the gentle articulation.

Breathing. I'd watch my belly rise as I inhaled air, filling my lungs to capacity. I'd pause and let the air release twice as slowly.

Circulation. I'd turn my world upside down physically and mentally. First, with a handstand against the wall to get blood pumping to my self-sabotaging brain. Then, I'd rephrase the negative uneasiness into a positive attestation, thinking of all the ways this was going *right*.

And when I needed more support, I had an online community to fall back on. When two or more entrepreneur physicians get together, there's unspoken empathy to draw strength from. But when a league of us gather online, imposter syndrome can't possibly survive in our presence. We traded our insecurities like playing cards to help each other win a better hand in the next round. We'd ask for feedback often and give advice. Soon, I had an elite tribe of resources from accountants to attorneys to window washers.

While the Near-Death Experience brought clarity, it was the energy from New-Relationship Energy that propelled me forward. Head over heels in love with innovative medical care, I was creating quite the dazzling brochure all on my own.

CHAPTER TWENTY-FOUR

SOLITARY CONFINEMENT

One of the first assignments on an entrepreneur physician's agenda is to pick a business name. As expected, the permanence of this decision created instant uncertainty. Like baking a perfectionistic cake. Hours were wasted, searching for a name that was tasteful and decadent. I wanted something that rolled off the tongue and empowered patients, all in one morsel. Eventually, I just had to throw it in the oven and bake it at 350° F.

There are times when cakes and creativity land flat.

"That must be so…*hard*." This woman's eyes held a trace of empathy, yet her mouth was downturned.

It was my first medical conference as a *solo* practitioner. I'd been seeing patients in my new office for several months and was no longer enslaved to the System. At this conference, I was faced with a deliciously new and difficult decision. I couldn't decide which shiny new label to write on my name tag: Founder. Owner. CEO. President. It didn't matter. They all felt ablaze with pride. I was proof that there was another way.

"I'm sorry, I don't understand?" I questioned. I wondered if her comment pertained to the "Functional Medicine" label on my nametag, as it was not yet widespread terminology to some medical professionals.

She dragged the plastic stir stick around the edge of her coffee, mixing the creamer while shaking her head. "I just don't know how you do it," she added.

"Actually, I really enjoy my job. Functional medicine is a breath of fresh air," I defended.

She smiled politely and turned to face the newest distraction in line: a towering giant of a man next to her, wearing a name tag scrawled with black Sharpie, "DR. JAMES ERICKSON, HOLLYWOOD'S *TOP* GASTROENTEROLOGIST."

It must take a special ego to yearn to be the top of the bottoms.

I shrugged and reached for a deviled egg, accidentally bumping into another physician wearing a Green Bay Packers polo.

"Hey! Cheesehead! I live in Wisconsin, too!" I thrust my hand to meet his. He shook it, and we started the usual Wisconsin comparisons: how many deer were dodged on the drive to the airport, how far below zero will our winter temperatures fall.

Then he glanced down at my name tag and sighed with heavy eyes. "Wow. I don't know how ya do it. I could never do your job."

He popped a cocktail sausage in his mouth and chomped, "I mean…day in and *day out*? That kinda patient demographic would wear on me, ya know? And being a woman?! That's gotta be even tougher."

Before I could decide if I was offended or perplexed, a third doctor overheard his thick Wisconsin accent and turned to greet us. A spritely pixie, she enthusiastically chirped a well-rehearsed introduction, "Hi, I'm from Chippewa Falls (yes, the same town that Jack was from in the movie *Titanic*)!" She went on to describe her time as an Air Force medic, deployed to Afghanistan in 2003. She paused mid-sentence as she read my name tag.

"But at least my assignment was only twelve months. Sheesh. I can't imagine doing *your* job…like, forever?!" She shook her head and patted her hand firmly on my shoulder. "Thank you for your efforts. Please. Be safe."

I was baffled.

Dr. James Erickson, Hollywood's "Top" Gastroenterologist, pivoted his six-foot-six frame to peer over our discussion. He clutched his scotch, and the ice clinked protectively in the snifter. Abruptly, Doc Hollywood hinged at the waist, bringing his sour face within millimeters to squint at my name tag.

He huffed loudly, feigning disinterest. "So are you serving the federal or state prison systems?"

"WHAT?!" I gasped. They all nodded to my name tag with their eyes. Collectively, they peered uncomfortably closer to my chest.

Air Force Amy breathed a sigh of relief. "Ohhhhhhhh! The *name* of your private practice is Health *Innate*. I thought it said Health *INMATE*."

It all made sense. It was then I understood why my office inbox was getting flooded with voice messages from state penitentiary recruiters.

CHAPTER TWENTY-FIVE
ADULTING 201

"And what do we do when we've survived another week of *working motherhood*?!" a voice shrieked above the group of friends huddled in a booth for our "Girls' Night Out" at a local restaurant. Voices echoed in unison: "We *drink*!"

Glasses flanked with glossy manicured nails rose high into the air as murmurs of deadlines, playdates, and school projects began. I shared the story of my regretfully hilarious business name.

"Hey, maybe you could really lean into that prison theme!" someone exclaimed. "It could be cute: striped couch cushions and signs like 'Don't let sugar be your ball and chain!'"

The waitress passed through, taking drink orders. I smiled and shook my head as my friend interrupted:

"Wait, what? *You don't want a glass of Cab*?" There was a collective gasp. One friend broke the tension with hushed tones, "I mean, it's *Girls' Night*. We *always* reward ourselves with drinks! Wait—" She glanced furtively across the cluster of heads. "Do you have a *problem* we should know about?"

Six pairs of eyes turned to await my response. I laughed. Careful to assemble my words, I reassured the group, "No. Not at all. I'm just learning a lot about what I prefer to spend my energy on—"

"So you're saying you'd rather *not* be here with *us*?" another friend pouted with her velvet matte lip.

"No, no. That's not what I meant!" My face flushed. I suddenly realized what I was up against. I lived in Wisconsin. There was a standard expectation that every adult citizen should have a weekend BAC above the legal limit.

I continued, "With all these new things to learn, running my own practice and all, I noticed I was feeling more anxious. I had developed a habit of 'relaxing' with a glass of wine with dinner. But I started to notice I always felt tired the next day. And if I drank two glasses, I was tired *and anxious*. So, one week I tried skipping the wine and felt my mood rise. Then, one week turned into eight months and now I feel absolutely boundless with energy."

They stared, unblinking and befuddled. For good reason. I temporarily forgot where we were standing. All around the bar, signs hung on the walls, proudly boasting our position as the drunkest state in America: "Drink Wisconsibly" and "Small town, big drinking problem." Likewise, I ascribed to this culture when we moved here. I was first to coordinate an impromptu night of blurry dancing, celebrating whatever festival was on tap: Oktoberfest, Christmas, St. Patrick's Day, 2 p.m. on a Saturday.

As a primary care doctor, I even selectively agreed with the supporting research proclaiming benefits of cardiac health and longevity (but discarded the mounting evidence of increased dementia, fatty liver, and breast cancer).

I continued, "In medical school, we were taught that alcoholism is an all-or-nothing diagnosis. We overlooked the majority of us that aced that screening questionnaire, but had a dysfunctional relationship with alcohol. Many of us use alcohol to socially connect, but individually, we're feeling a constant hum of anxiety or daily headaches and poor sleep. I'm telling ya, when you experiment without it, and you feel so good, you question all the societal marketing of adulthood."

The mumbling quieted, but the slow sipping continued.

I softened my words a bit. "If you think about it, there's really no medicinal use for alcohol. It's basically a legal poison. I'll still drink on rare occasions, but now I prepare for the fallout using functional medicine principles. I'll support my gastrointestinal tract with L-glutamine, eat more leafy greens to power up my mitochondria, and take some N-acetyl cysteine with milk thistle to support my liver the next day. Listen, the bottom line is: I'm really excited to see *you* tonight. I'll support whatever makes you feel sparkly, so I'll raise my glass of *sparkling water* to cheer you on!"

Satisfied, they nodded their heads and we clinked. Maybe it's not alcohol we crave, but the sound of glasses clinking in solidarity.

"I'm not sure I can do *that*," another voice proclaimed from our group.

I shrugged my shoulders. She continued, "No. I'm not talking about wine. I'm talking about *this*." Her poppy red fingernail pointed at someone else's unattended cell phone resting face down. Yet another faux "connection" visible in today's society: technology. While the rest of the group scrolled and sipped, the owner of the cell phone perked up.

This femme rebel of 3G thrust her phone up in the air with disdain. "We're distracted all day long with notifications, buzzes, and beeps. I found myself attached to this *damn thing*. I'd respond without thinking, and I was giving everything else my half-ass attention." She stabbed grilled salmon with her fork while the rest of us looked up.

Measuring our doubtful glares, she may as well have been churning butter in an Amish farmhouse. Now it was her turn at the pulpit.

"Remember when we used to wait for Must See Thursday TV?! We'd all gush about it at work the next day, talking about the episodes the night before. It gave us connection. We had community. But *now*, it's *binge all you want* on Netflix on your own timeline. Keep scrolling on YouTube for hours. Count up those 'likes.' Distraction instead of attraction. No connection with the people right in front of you!"

I surveyed the room.

Everyone's fingers were pecking at their phones like acrylic hens.

One woman piped up, "But I love technology and social media! It's helped me rekindle a friendship with one of my high school classmates I lost touch with!"

I joined the chorus, "I'm sorry, but I just can't *not* pay attention to my phone. I mean, it's my calling. My job. I run my own private medical practice now. They're *expecting* me to respond. People want constant communication, and I feel like I *have* to be available twenty-four/seven."

Rebel 3G sarcastically sneered. "C'mon. What emergencies happen in a *holistic* medical practice on a Thursday at 7 p.m.? Meditation session went too deep? Coffee enema gone wrong? Or, for that matter, what emergencies truly happen in our relationships or life that make us obsessively check our texts? If something is *that* bad, they'll *actually* call you or they'll go to the ER!"

Good point.

One by one, we meekly turned our phones to silent and overturned them on the tabletop. An hour passed and no one touched their phones, which meant we were officially spiritual gangstas. We tossed cash on the table to pay the bill and gathered up our belongings.

As everyone resumed their scrolling and pecking, I turned on my phone to reveal five texts and four missed calls from CJ.

"Oh my God," I gasped. We slowly rose from the table in apprehension.

I played the message on speaker as we listened to CJ recount his ER visit with Emery, finally concluding: "Thankfully, all the tests so far revealed simple indigestion for her abdominal pain. No appendicitis. Enjoy your dinner with the ladies and we'll see you at home soon."

"Wow. Spoken like a doc. Unflappable," murmured someone.

"Proof that we do need our phones," said another, throwing a daggered stare at Rebel 3G. The waitress began wiping the table and added with a wink, "I don't care what you crazies say, I'm not giving up my beer *or* phone."

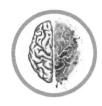

CHAPTER TWENTY-SIX

PASSING THE PLATE

Life would be easier if we had an on/off switch to mark our roles and labels. White coat on: doctor mode. Sunscreen on: running mode. Earplugs in: road trip is on—*but not listening to your bickering, so help me God.*

Determined to find a better solution, I announced the On-Call Parent (OCP) system. A colorful bandana would serve as a visual signal that was friendlier than a pager, but just as necessary. I was confident this would solve all in-home traffic problems.

Can't find the remote? Wondering where the jar of peanut butter went? Want to voice your complaint about the unjust amount of extra time your sibling had on Xbox? Ask the parent wearing the bandana.

Unfortunately, the invisible umbilical cord attached to a mother is stronger than any cloth-signalling system. Like blind, determined homing pigeons, our kids would step past the On-Call Parent chopping food in the kitchen. They would march their trek across the living room, check behind a minimum of three doors, proceed down the stairs to locate my laundry-folding position in a remote basement area. Just to ask, "What's for dinner?"

During those initial years as an employed conventional doctor, it was easy to shed the white coat before coming home.

I'd leave it hanging at the darkened clinic until 8 a.m. the next morning when the staff and I started our routine over again. When that coat was off, I was no longer a doctor, and free to disconnect my medical brain.

I staunchly believe that every doctor mom needs access to three different white coats, each with its own justification. The first should be equally generic and boxy. When worn properly, it should possess the insipid personality of a first date with a statistician. It's utilitarian purpose is to simply complete the doctor costume. The second coat serves as a roomy white tent, large enough to smuggle nine months of burgeoning pregnant belly underneath. It is an upscale equivalent of a house dress (minus the hair rollers and fuzzy slippers). The final white coat is the mainstay of medical feminism as it delivers welcome reprieve to the tired doctor mom. A delicately cinched waist creates a stylish silhouette, enough so one could wear a spit-up-stained burlap sack underneath and still feel acceptably chic.

As the years went on in family medicine, something suspicious began happening to my beloved collection of white coats. They felt altered after they returned from the hospital dry cleaners. Heavier. Stickier. No matter if I hung it up after a long workday, I could still feel it on my body. I couldn't find any lead in the pockets or new Velcro sewn in the lining. My white coat felt permanently attached as I spent more time typing on patients' charts every night. No different than my other colleagues who spent evenings under the glow of a laptop, since the average family physician spends eighty-six minutes of "pajama time"[9] every evening doing computer work.

When I left conventional employment to open my private practice, I thought this kind of after-hours work was behind me. I folded my white coats and stored them in my past, next to yearbooks with eighties perms and stonewashed jeans. Now, I was free in the middle of the day to volunteer for recess duty or bump grocery carts in the afternoon with the silvery AARP crowd. I had a schedule capable of meeting the cable guy anywhere between 10 a.m. to 8 p.m. Time was under my command.

No one warned me that autonomy comes with a 24/7 soundtrack.

I had exchanged my solo melody of "physician" with an orchestra of cacophony. Instead of the disengaged ballad performed in F minor, I had a high-tempo jazz improv of unpredictable stress. So many players: entrepreneur, graphic designer, copywriter, educator, speaker, marketer, community philanthropist. It seemed I always had eight refrains going simultaneously, without intermission.

This Private-Practice Polka would interrupt my sleep with impromptu concerts:

> *It just snowed four inches* again. *I need to shovel my office sidewalk before someone slips.*
> *Is my seventy-six-question intake form too complicated?*
> *Why is my Facebook ad getting rejected again?*

Ah. This must be the new flavor of my shit sandwich. Goodbye, burnout. Hello, overwhelm.

As the conductor of this musical, I needed assistance and I was hopelessly out of practice. The last time I asked for help was fourteen years ago.

"Hi, my husband is in Iraq, and I brought cookies." As soon as the words escaped my lips, I realized how hard it was to make friends as an adult. I tried again, "Welcome to the neighborhood!"

It was 2003, right after CJ had just boarded the plane to Iraq. Like an atrophied muscle, my friendship skills had withered. For the last half of a decade, all my friends were effortlessly identified by convenience: college roommates, medical students, residents. Now they were scattered across the nation, and I was alone with a boisterous toddler in an unfamiliar city, stationed outside of Fort Leonard Wood, Missouri.

I needed authentic support to survive this deployment as a solo working mom. After bathtime and lullabies, under the crackle of a baby monitor, I'd scroll through local community events and virtual bulletin boards online. Lit by the blue glow of my computer screen, I searched for nightly clues on where other adults found camaraderie and friendship. How do adults make friends, anyway?

It became shockingly clear that finding a convenient friend wasn't an online activity. Certainly not on the AdultFriendFinder. com website, where one needed to be "thirsty and available." Added to this impossible task, I inherited centuries of hardwired Finnish introversion. We have a cultural allergy to asking for help. The Finns pride themselves on independence and grit in the face of adversity. They even have a name for it: *sisu*.

It would require metric tons of *sisu* to physically crawl out of this isolation to make a friend. In person. Without the aid of my jovial husband. All by myself.

The universe must have heard my plea. Less than twenty-four hours later, I spied a familiar military moving truck pulling into our cul-de-sac. Eighteen minutes and 350 degrees later, I thrust a plate of warm chocolate chip cookies into my new neighbors' unsuspecting hands before they could hang up their camouflage uniforms.

The military taught families to be experts at zen nonattachment. We relished the depth of every moment because the general commander could change our weekend plans within a single sentence. During the next few months, I enjoyed the company of my new neighbors, bonding with them over our shared experiences.

Everything became a meaningful celebration. Beyond the usual trick-or-treating, Easter eggs, and birthdays, we took care of each other with the only currency we all have in this world: attention. I'd give curbside medical recommendations for a scraped knee, and they'd make sure my lawn never grew over two inches. After particularly long days at work, we'd sit under the summer night sky in our driveways, baby monitors crackling to compete with the police scanner (rural Missouri did not disappoint).

Nothing is more "Americana" than two military families raising young children in a quiet neighborhood off Old Route 66. Every evening, we'd drive our kids into the cookie-cutter subdivision. The only unusual part was that our exit ramp was conveniently marked by a glaring spotlight, circling the air, alerting truckers to the strip club across the highway. We needed an iconic explanation to explain this phenomenon to our preschooler. To this day, our oldest is proud to have lived across from the watchful eye of Batman and his Bat Signal.

Military life taught me the only two lessons needed on this earth:

1. Words matter. Direct and literal communication is important. When the military is ordered to "pack everything in sight" for your change of station, this includes unemptied trash with all its rotten fruit and maggots.

2. Control is an illusion. Everything changes in life. Adaptation is key.

When CJ returned home from deployment, he stepped into an unrecognizable world. We had all transformed to accommodate new people in our lives. He had new comrades that endured the same events in Iraq, and I had increased our home by 2,000 square feet (thanks to a well-worn path between our new military neighbors' door and our own).

As we adapted to our new lives, we learned that no two people should stay the same within the container of a relationship. Whether we showed up with open curiosity or closed assumptions determined everything. A relationship's success is not measured in the number of sunsets shared, but rather the number of recurring "First Dates" we have with upgraded versions of each other. One person cannot possibly fulfill every role. And when the world is a deluge of hardship, we need to seek out others.

Decades later, I was recognizing this same agitated feeling standing in my new office. On the surface, I had assembled my ideal world within my clinic: walls were adorned with colorful artwork and comfortable couches were intentionally placed for best feng shui. Educational binders, handouts, and dry-erase boards expressed the beauty of our ornate physiology. My office was brimming with healing and teaching. A feat accomplished by my own hard work.

But instead of pride, I felt the dread of overwhelm.

It was missing something crucial.

I needed to find neighbors. I needed to create a new well-worn path between other like-minded people that could help sharpen my direction and purpose. I needed to find a league of people who understood. Those neighbors that would permit me to collapse on their couches at the end of a long workday, offering solace and guidance just like my military friends. As a neophyte medical entrepreneur, I started preheating my metaphorical oven for the plate of virtual cookies I would offer to the universe. I just had to find which door to knock on.

And that's exactly what I found in the *Evolution of Medicine's Practice Accelerator*.

CHAPTER TWENTY-SEVEN
MUBER DUTY

This time, I wasn't trading cookies.

The gift that medical entrepreneurs exchange is *synergy*.

The *Evolution of Medicine's Practice Accelerator* provided the necessary framework to build a holistic model of medical care. Drs. Jeffrey Bland and Mark Hyman proved long ago that functional medicine could alleviate the burden of chronic disease in the late 1990s. Yet this kind of medical perspective was still isolated to the elite academic centers in larger cities. Functional medicine needed a viable method that allowed disbursement for those of us without large support staff and multiple phone lines. James Maskell's *Practice Accelerator* was a brilliant linchpin in the future of holistic medical care gone rogue.

Inside this online school, we learned how to effectively use technology to ease our entrepreneurial struggles. From picking the best electronic health records to marketing our unique strengths, we acquired the basics needed to support a thriving modern medical practice. We shared our ideas, practiced our video skills, and brainstormed in accountability groups.

As invigorating as this energy could be, my creative outpouring needed quiet balance. It's easy to feel all yin with no yang. All decent growth requires moments of pause and reflection. And I needed routine breaks to keep my ideas fresh. A pattern interrupt.

Mine happened at 3:14 p.m. every day.

Muber duty time. Mom + Uber = Muber.

Buses were vetoed by our oldest, Owen, when he discovered that our remote home address meant daily fifty-minute bus rides each way. We tried again with Emery and Beckett, but that only furthered their education on homemade shanks and explicit anatomical nouns.

With the advent of my flexible office hours, our kids graduated from a bus to a Muber.

As a fledgling entrepreneur, tense with perpetual overwhelm, I initially met this Muber intrusion with exasperation. My Muber light was on 24/7, but the busiest hours were from 3 to 5 p.m. Pick-up and drop-off locations could change within a thirty-second text. Soon, I realized the boon of this ritual. It forced a rhythm to my day, something I desperately needed.

Similar to Uber, I never knew what state my passengers would be in: angry, hypoglycemic, staggering from existential angst. I rolled up silently to the curb, observing the crest of students flooding from the middle school doors. I braced myself and clutched the steering wheel as the doors opened. Taking a deep breath, I inhaled Taylor Swift's "You Need to Calm Down" like it was fresh oxygen.

Muber experiences did *not* start with the usual pleasantries: "Hi, Uber for Tony? Yes! How's your afternoon going?" I also did not supply bottles of spring water or mints.

Instead, my Muber experience started with high-decibel commands like, "How come you *never* have food in here?!" or "Okay, so here's the plan: we need to get groceries *right now* because fifteen friends are coming over for a sleepover in twenty minutes."

I chanted my mantra over and over: *Emotions are contagious. Emotions are contagious. Emotions are contagious.*

Despite all my best efforts to channel my inner Gandhi, I failed. My voice reflected the current mood of the ride, and I shrieked, "Put your seatbelt on *please*," and followed with "I don't keep food in here because *you* don't pick up the wrappers and my car looks like a motorized napkin!"

Muber jobs are paramount and essential, albeit somewhat disrespected. On-the-job training helped me to develop a serene poker face. But sometimes it was *too* poker-y, and I would be asked why I was "always in a bad mood."

Although it sounds death-defying and scary, a Muber experience can blossom into a memorable ride. My tiny car carried some ginormous conversations with titles like, "Why Does My Fourth-Grade Classmate Have a Mustache Already?" and "Let Me Tell You All About My Dreams to Become a YouTuber." I've had miraculous glimpses into my kids' lives that only happened with this recipe of forced communication.

Or not.

Muber passengers could also be weirdly silent. I learned not to sing, talk, ask, joke, or interrupt their thoughts with attempts of banter or inquiry, especially between the ages of ten and fifteen. It's best to leave them be. They're temporarily lost in the swirl of puberty.

That day, I was defiant. Still high on the blossoming creative thoughts I had when forced to truncate my day, I had an idea.

As Emery slumped into the car, I barked in a circus voice: "Muber price surge! Due to high-demand hours!"

Her face imploded into a disdainful pucker. "What?" she sneered.

I continued, transforming this spectacle into my most overly-enunciated, polished British accent, "Dueeee to the high demand of transportation, there will be an extra charge today, Miss!"

Her eyes rolled. She absentmindedly reached for her phone, then recoiled reflexively. This was one unbreakable and imperative rule of Muber rides: don't even think about touching your cell phone. I don't care if you sit in silence with steam huffing through flared nostrils, but smiling and stroking your phone like a pet is not allowed during daily routine trips.

I continued, deadpan, "You need to provide two facts about yourself that I don't already know. Then you have permission to ride in this Muber."

In the disarray of motherhood, shared transportation provided a unique opportunity to learn about my brood. How else would I have heard lovely gems like this from a young six-year-old Beckett: "Hey, Mom, did you know that love will never go away? Because God is inside love!" Or played the frivolous game "Guess how many times Mommy thought of you today?!" (The answer was always "infinity.")

Muber conversations like these were priceless.

Emery: "Well, here's something; I'm not good at spelling. We had a spelling bee today and I got out on a *four-letter* word."

Me: "Aw, sweetie. That's okay. Spelling bees *are* hard. What word did you miss?"

Emery: "Minor."

Me: "That's a five-letter word."

Emery: "Oh yeah, and I'm also not good at math."

If time is the only currency we have, Muber duty helped me become the ultimate Wall Street stock trader junkie. I learned to capitalize on where I spent my precious time and energy dividends. A lot could be learned on the way to middle school. Likewise, if I arranged my day purposefully, I could access useful ideas faster and easier.

I became used to having radical concepts emerge at unusual times: after a shower, during a run, or driving in the car. With this newfound creativity incontinence, I was forced to find new ways of containing and organizing my information. I'd talk to myself on a voice memo, scribble on a dry-erase board by the shower, or doodle on mini-notebooks in my purse. No surface area was safe. Two-ply toilet paper proved sturdy enough to handle the aftermath of family taco night as well as ballpoint outlines for a new patient handout.

Creativity seemed to obey the first law of thermodynamics: it's neither created or destroyed. It's transformed energy. Einstein agreed, "A problem can't be solved with the same level of thinking that created it." Creative ideas aren't entirely original. They feed on the mutual brainstorming of others.

Working alongside other medical entrepreneurs in this online *Practice Accelerator* community, we could be vulnerable in ways that we couldn't otherwise. It was a resurgence of a virtual doctor's lounge of sorts. We'd celebrate book launches, course creations, and patient success stories. We'd lament over the stodgy and slow-moving wheels of conventional medicine unwilling to adopt our methods. We'd exchange tips on the best technology to use in our unique practices.

Just like the clockwork routine of Muber duty, we passed the plate of flavorful "cookies" every day. We became each other's daily dose of support and inspiration to combat the paralysis of overwhelm.

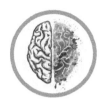

CHAPTER TWENTY-EIGHT

KREPLITS RISING

"If we are wise in our energy management, we find that ideas emerge when we least expect them. Our minds are constantly working in the background to solve whatever problems we give them. We just need to be strategic about clearing the way and ensuring they have the energy they need to do their job. It's amazing what happens when we work with, rather than against, the natural flow of the creative process." —Todd Henry, author of *The Accidental Creative.*

Finding my natural creative flow was as easy as coaxing my children to get up for the third day of school. (The first day of school is like winning the morning lottery: they bounce out of bed and into their carefully assembled outfits and scuff-free shoes. It's the third day where reality sets in and speed limits become roadside suggestions.) I stumbled into my fourth decade before acknowledging that "energy management" was critical to surviving any chapter of working motherhood. Even more necessary with entrepreneurship.

Kreplits (a term originally coined by educator Kidder Kaper in regard to managing relationships and self-care) signify a unit of time/energy and love/affection that you give yourself and others. For most of my life, I had mindlessly dispensed my kreplits like penny candy at a loud parade. Sweltering in the heat, I'd toss them off the rickety float and see who grabbed a spot on my agenda. I signed on for coffee dates, committee meetings, and family obligations in between work and life. Soon, my colorful Google calendar resembled a Pride celebration every month, except without the love and respect. My kreplits had no value. I was using currency that was tired, worn out, and ineffective.

It took a stock market crash in my own personal kreplit economy to realize I needed help.

I was having a stellar afternoon, packed full with patients and conference calls. I was keeping up with the hectic pace. I was "knocking it out of the park," as my father would say to me as a young child. (Having a daughter who was missing the "sports lobe" of the brain must have been frustrating for him to impart this baseball wisdom. He'd point his invisible bat into imaginary stands and swing with gusto to help me understand this "knocking" was apparently a good thing.)

It was a beautiful day in the medical entrepreneur neighborhood, indeed.

Until my phone rang.

"Your son missed his doctor's appointment," the receptionist explained. The sentence echoed in my skull. I *never* missed appointments. Not even the ones I *wanted* to miss (like "Jump Rope For Heart" in fourth grade. Even then, I was skeptical as to how my rope tripping could ease an octogenarian's angina attack. Yet I showed up). I had clearly forgotten to pick him up from school for this important event.

This was too much. Reality was jarring me to reassess my expense report. My profit/loss of kreplits was overdrawn, and my energy economy was suffering from unmonitored inflation.

I started revamping my spoken language first. I replaced passive phrases like "I don't have time" with more literal statements like "that's not a priority for me right now." I stopped sugar-coating with half-hearted agreements to join the latest club or fad fitness trend. I doubled down on building the value back on my kreplits. I started keeping track of where I spent my attention, as it directly cost precious brain energy. Only those requests that instantly filled my heart with love or inspiration deserved my prized kreplits.

As my priorities shifted, I realized this was more than simple time management. Rehabilitating my kreplit economy required looking squarely at my core values. Until then, I carelessly settled on values adopted from my family or friends like one would land on a lucky BINGO square. Achievement? *I got it!* Harmony? *Yes.* Compassion? *I got that one, too!*

I never stopped to think whether those specific values fit *my* goals. They all sounded adequate at the time. As a young twenty-something doctor, I depended on the scaffolding of stability, predictability, and routine. This complimented a life when other surprises could surface on a whim, like husband deployment or new babies. BINGO.

Then comfort had turned into conformity. Dependability dissolved into tediousness. And when I could no longer describe my career in family medicine without using words like "restrictive" and "claustrophobic," I knew something was amiss. No wonder the effortless transition into medical entrepreneurism felt less like a leap and more of a skip. I could relish my sparkly new core values of creativity, autonomy, and innovation. And yet, this persistent imbalance of time management was casting an obstructive shadow upon my new chapter of freedom.

While the receptionist was busy rescheduling my son's missed appointment, I was dumping my invisible, overstacked BINGO card for a fresh one. I could feel the excitement of an impending win. I was *almost* there. I just needed to develop a solid, consistent structure.

It is said we are an average of the five people we surround ourselves with. Seeking to right my imbalanced life, I sought the wisdom of Marie Kondo, Steve Jobs, Simon Sinek, Elizabeth Gilbert, and Brené Brown. I needed to explore another key ingredient of time management. Who better to learn from than the kreplit masters?

CHAPTER TWENTY-NINE

EVERYONE ELSE
IS DOING IT

"Dad, I think Mom is going crazy."

CJ continued chopping vegetables without acknowledging Owen's gaze. "Possibly. It's happened before. While Mom was on maternity leave with Emery, she watched hours of HGTV. I came home one evening to find that Mom painted an 'accent wall' in our bathroom. It was *matte black*. She insisted that it was to 'unify and anchor the space.' It was so black it sucked universes into orbit. Our neighbors' dishes trembled on their dinner table."

I emerged from the bedroom, mounds of clothes dripping off my arms, head held high, with an air of defiance. "I was just experimenting! I didn't realize it would be that horrid. In my defense, I did return it to the original color within seventy-two hours," I huffed.

Emery watched silently between scoops of oatmeal.

"What are you doing with your clothes? Is this about you boycotting bedroom furniture?" Owen asked.

"Dressers *are* a waste of space!" I retorted. "We live in laundry limbo ninety-nine percent of the time when clothes never make it to their dresser drawers. We should just have two baskets of clothes in the laundry room: dirty and clean-but-musty because someone inevitably forgot to put them in the dryer days ago."

I paused to pick up a pilly cardigan from the floor. "No, this is not about dressers. *This* is something more. Bigger. It's going to improve my brain power!" I felt the beads of sweat forming on my brow. "All the top entrepreneurs and CEOs do this," I proclaimed, my voice muffled as I descended to the basement with my third pile of clothes.

I had removed other unhelpful variables in my kreplit equation: that nightly glass of wine that turned my daytime fatigue up a notch. Those bland events that required excessive small talk and no real connection. Now I spoke with directness that often startled my Midwest friends and family, using astonishing phrases like "No, thank you."

"Hey, Mom? Which do you like better: sunrise or sunset?" Beckett interrupted, off topic. He was always a flurry of incongruent thoughts and wonderings, as if completing an infinite crossword puzzle in his mind.

"I'm bi-sun. I love both," I answered absentmindedly.

Beckett continued, "Okay, so what *are* you really doing there?"

I dropped my garment mound and explained, "Okay, there's this thing called *decision fatigue*. Our brains get tired as the day goes on, so thinking becomes harder. Willpower fades quicker. If you ask me to let you have donuts for breakfast at 7 a.m., I'll say no because my brain is well rested and full of energy. I'll even be able to explain my good reasons. But have you noticed that when I'm on Muber duty later that day at 3 p.m., tired after a long day at work, I'll cave in. You'll get the donut."

Beckett may be the curious explorer of the mind, but Emery was the expert at zeroing in on blunt facts to get to the point: "Okay. But why are you boxing up all your clothes?"

"I've been reading about how the most effective thought leaders had ways to protect their energy. Most had strict morning routines that allowed their brain to go on autopilot, saving the important decisive thinking for bigger things at work. They'd eat, exercise, meditate, and journal all before their work day started."

Silence.

"So I'm looking to remove tiny decisions that could tire my brain out!" My enthusiasm crescendoed as I disappeared. I shouted from the bedroom, "Ready? Here comes my *big reveal*!"

I barked, "*Behold*! My new uniform!"

Then I reappeared wearing a crisp white blouse and gray pants. Emery wrinkled her nose and dropped her spoon into the empty bowl with a loud clink. "Yeah, Mom is *definitely* going crazy."

CJ glanced up. "Really? That's *all* you will wear? Like every single day?"

"Do not question my brilliance!" I told him, then boasted, "Now my mornings will be even more effortless! I won't waste my precious energy on fashion choices!"

"I had no idea that getting dressed in the morning was so utterly taxing for you." CJ smirked.

"Mom, you look like a janitor." Emery shook her head.

CHAPTER THIRTY

BITE THE HAND

The very next morning, I was vacuuming my waiting room in my not-so-ironic custodian uniform. If you would've asked me a decade ago about going into private practice, I would've rattled off a list of pessimistic reasons not to: Who will get the faxes? Answer phones? Take out the trash? Clean the counters? Forward all the inbox messages and refills? Who will wipe down all the doorknobs?!!!

This is the occult indoctrination of the modern medical school fairytale. After an arduous day scrubbing the castle floors on our knees, we are tucked into bed every night with harrowing tales about the futility of an independent practice. Meanwhile, our dental, naturopathic, and chiropractic colleagues roam the countryside on their private-practice stallions.

It was easy to absorb this conditioning, since becoming a physician was already a treacherous, upward climb of promises. We were perpetually tired. For me, it began on a Friday at 2 a.m. in college while I was up memorizing cellular respiration, and my college roommate was almost home from the pub crawl. "It will get better...*once I get into medical school*," I told myself.

Fast-forward to medical school, and I was up at 2 a.m. again, cramming every dose of prescription antibiotics and antifungals into my memory to pass the first of many board exams. "It will get better...*once I'm done with all these tests*."

A few years later, I walked the hospital halls like a zombie with a belt of pagers, waiting for a catastrophe to happen during my tenth on-call shift that month. "It will get better...*once I'm done with this call.*"

By that time, I was addicted to promises. I figured that once I was out in the "real world" with extra staff, a new EMR roll-out, hospital rebuild, and incentives like branded umbrellas and embossed luggage tags, that things would be different. "It will get better...*once I can close my panel to new patients.*"

This is the missing class in medical school: Empty Promises 101. Our curriculum already contained courses like histology, anatomy, microbiology, and pathology. But there was no preparation for the bleak future of factory healthcare when a physician suddenly realized the truth: it *doesn't* get better. Our world was an enteric-coated lie, souring in our stomachs. Medical school may have taught us the skills to deftly spot signs of decay and death, but it ignored the rotting within our own healthcare system—lest we bite the royal hand that fed us.

American healthcare had an exponential increase in administrative jobs[10] compared to physicians. Over the years, endless pseudo-titles popped up like antagonists in our medical fairy tale: Coach, Manager, Director, Special Project Manager, Consultant, Coordinator. Meanwhile, the main heroes of healthcare, the physicians, had flatlined in their growth. And we wonder why we have the most expensive healthcare in the world.

As physicians are stretched thinner with ridiculous mandates and compliance checklists, malpractice cases increase[11]. No longer able to rely on adequate supporting staff, this forces physicians to click their computer mouse an average of 4,000 times[12]. Electronic medical records previously intended on improving safety for patients now increase rates of disability and death due to mistakes in EMR[13].

Traditional hospital administration leads this hollow war to dominate the healthcare kingdom. Employed primary care physicians must fall in line, so they are restricted in expressing their particular approach or tech tools they prefer. It's impossible to allow unique styles to emerge in patient care without passing approval from the royal court of department heads, administrative committees, and branch managers. Those original values of trust, health, and personalization at the root of medical care have been replaced by a prior-authorized court jester.

As it turned out, wearing the same clothes every day had the opposite effect on my creativity and did not free up any extra bandwidth of energy. After several months, I exhumed my previous wardrobe from storage. I was searching for kreplits in the wrong place. The answer to my entrepreneurial angst was not in my closet. It wasn't even in my own brain.

It was in the ether of technology.

This plot twist to becoming a rogue physician was the epitome of irony. Medical school didn't teach complex business skills because doctors don't need complex business skills. It was shockingly simple to operate a lean, private micropractice. Every solid decision passed through three screening questions:

1. Is this task requiring my highest level of expertise?

2. If not, which virtual space can handle it?

3. How can I repurpose my efforts for maximum reach?

Technology was the only essential coworker required. Google voice transcribed voicemail to my cell phone. Automated responses answered simple questions from free advertising on social media. Patients scheduled their own appointments with online calendars. Email nurture sequences explained the onboarding process. HIPAA-compliant electronic medical records charged pennies per chart from a secure cloud platform, accessible anywhere. Comprehensive patient education could be recorded and saved in an online academy. Patients learned about their lab results from password-protected videos that recorded my interpretations, making their follow-up visits more impactful and efficient.

No wonder physicians were burned out in the traditional healthcare model. They couldn't advance past the first screening question. They were not using their highest level of expertise within the castle walls. Instead, their absurd list of tasks grew longer on their royal decree. On a shoestring budget, it was possible to lower the drawbridge and walk out. Providing a solo medical practice that delivered excellence in a rural community was entirely possible when you built your own kingdom.

CHAPTER THIRTY-ONE
STEP RIGHT UP

"Hi, I don't see your menu posted. Do you serve chai latte with almond milk?" the woman asked.

This was the third time someone entered my office that afternoon, inquiring about fair-trade coffee. The sun was shining, the warm summer breeze fluttered the storekeepers' awnings. Fresh produce and colorful merchandise was proudly displayed on the sidewalks. Mothers with strollers and curious dog walkers waved at each other. It was these days that our quintessential Midwest downtown square shined in Norman Rockwell glory.

I aimed to "color outside the lines" of a typical doctor's office, and as a result, my office resembled a hip, neighborhood coffee shop. This time, I skipped the bizarre HGTV suggestions and took my inspiration for interior design from Gandhi. "Be the change you want to see in the world." The method was simple. Whenever I was faced with a decision on decor, I'd ask myself, *What would a hospital do?* And then I'd do the opposite.

It was not unusual for a passerby to notice the colorfully painted skeleton in the window and saunter in to gaze at the artwork. I was proud of this whimsical museum where medicine met art. Between shifts of Muber duty, I'd offer a guided tour to anyone who visited.

I started their expedition with the *literal* end in mind: the bathroom. Much of the research in functional medicine revolves around the gut and proper elimination, so the throne must be royal in this new kingdom. The farmhouse sink was surrounded with a resin-topped floating vanity made from repurposed barn wood in Wisconsin. On the wall was my "Table of Essential Elements," eight painted, square canvases arranged in a geometric fashion featuring the expected *Carbon, Oxygen, Nitrogen* and their corresponding molecular weights. I included other important elements like *Broccoli (Br) and Exercise (Ex)*. *Love (Lo)* had a molecular weight of 365 days per year, of course.

The final "essential" element hanging in the bathroom was the *Cell Phone (Cp)*. Only those born before 1980 will recognize the molecular weight of *Cell Phone (Cp)* as Tommy Tutone's 867-5309.

The next stop on the tour was the exam room. Depending on perspective, it was either a cozy area where I taught patients about the inner workings of their bodies or evidence of the intensity of IFM certification. The far wall was painted in floor-to-ceiling dry-erase paint, displaying the contents of my studying. It was crawling with abundantly intricate drawings of the biochemical processes of human physiology. Purple neurons with dopamine and serotonin. A red cardiac heart with homocysteine, folate, and Coenzyme Q10. Orange intestinal tissue spurting forth secretory Immunoglobulin A and zonulin. Tiny arrows and letters scrawling the expansive wall demonstrated how magnificently colorful and complex our beautiful bodies are.

The final stop was the waiting room. It was not much of a "waiting" room, but rather a "learning" room where I hosted workshops and open office hours. Designed with comfort and collaboration in mind, it was unsurprising that this room was mistaken for a cafe—or, as my kids thought of it, an alternate surface to leave crumbs or forgotten homework. The north wall functioned as an artistic parade, from Factory Doctor to Free Physician. We started in front of a giant three-foot square canvas, paper mâchéd with faded sheet music from my high school band years. Over top was painted a bold green circle, left open ended.

"This is a Japanese ensō, signifying enlightenment and totality of the universe," I clarified.

"Or it's the circling sign of death when your internet is buffering in the WiFi of farmland," she giggled.

"Same!" I shrugged.

Flanked to the right was a wooden board, hand-painted with an alabaster silhouette of Wisconsin. A tiny crimson heart was placed at the location of our hometown, Monroe.

"That's so sweet!" she remarked, "Isn't the motto 'America's Hometown'?"

"No. Actually, Monroe's motto is 'We Bring You Back,' but I didn't think that painting a boomerang would be as idyllic."

The largest art installation was a three-foot upside-down, tear-drop-shaped map icon. Made from thick home insulation sealed with seafoam resin, it was an easily recognizable shape. But instead of the usual "You are here," below the icon, it boldly challenged, "Are you here?" A reminder to be grounded in presence, aligned within yourself, regardless of physical location.

"I wanted my art to include moments that are familiar to all of us, since we all have similar paths," I explained. "But I also like hiding a bit of embarrassing humor."

I pointed to a long, white corrugated plaque, horizontally placed at eye level. A teal waveform stretched across the middle axis. "This is something for my kids. This image is the sound wave that is produced when your voice says the word *puberty.*"

Whenever a teen rolls their eyes, mothers across the world glow a little brighter with power. It's a universal truth.

The guest chuckled. "I love it! This whole place, I mean. It's like Pinterest threw up on the walls."

"Exactly!" I walked to the finale and pointed to my favorite piece: a painted profile of the human head with antique gears for brains. It represented the brain fog of motherhood. Each location was identified with faux neuroanatomical labels like Superior Snooze Button Gyrus, Cerebellar Foci of Coffee, or Ventricle of Misplaced Keys.

The clock tower chimed the end of another afternoon. As the guest made her way to the door, she pointed to the psychedelic skeleton smiling in the window. "And who is this dapper fella?"

"Oh, that's Vinny! He's family. Originally a Halloween decoration, he underwent his own midlife transformation when I painted him to become the creative mascot of this space. He's a perfect ambassador for the art of medicine. Also, he's the best roommate I've ever had. Quiet, cheerful, and never makes a mess."

She thanked me for the tour, and I directed her down the block to a *real* coffee shop. I shut the door and flipped a "CLOSED" sign as I prepared my slides for that night's workshop.

CHAPTER THIRTY-TWO

CHECK YOUR PULSE

Pause.

And then a round of enthusiastic clapping.

From *three* pairs of hands.

I had just hosted my first group workshop to teach my rural community about intestinal permeability ("leaky gut") as the gateway to chronic disease. If "back pain" was the bread and butter of a family doctor's day, then "leaky gut" was the functional medicine equivalent. This low-level inflammation, when left unaddressed, could lead to a variety of chronic diseases like irritable bowel syndrome[14], autoimmune disease[15], parkinson's[16], and heart disease[17]. If I could educate my community and provide them with a handful of critical first steps, our collective health could be saved.

The three pairs of hands belonged to my friends.

It was like having your mom and her church ladies come to your TED talk. Obviously, I had some work to do to entice my community to learn. I was up against decades of disappointing experiences with conventional medicine: quick doctor visits without quality teaching or supportive behavior change. Every sentence was punctuated with the click of a mouse, instantly e-faxing a prescription to the nearest pharmacy.

I needed to prove that health education could be fun and interesting, rather than shameful and impossible. I wanted to bring back the *docere* in "doctor." When did the meaning of *health* and *care* get stripped from healthcare? Just like the incongruent term "busboy," I was neither a bus nor a boy at my first high school job, wiping tables and taking salad orders in an iconic and well-loved local pizza joint.

The decor was classic fifties-style diner with brightly mopped floors and shiny tables. Waiters smiled and fluttered about cheerfully, a stark contrast with the real truth behind the scenes. In the back kitchen stood a portly chef, his uniform covered in a sheen of grease, cigar hanging from his mouth, ashes dropping into the vat of ranch dressing below. I watched in horror as breadsticks would fall to the gritty floor and get scooped up by the wait staff, dropped in a plastic serving basket, and carried out of the kitchen. He'd triumphantly bellow, "Five-second rule!" each and every time.

"Salad" at that pizza joint was a contrived formality. Wilted lettuce and puckered cherry tomatoes weren't exactly phytonutrient-rich. And yet, there I was, placing the greens on a plate and scooping up ranch dressing, trying to avoid cigar ash. It felt like a false performance, an unnecessary waste. No one ever ate the salads. People came for the artery-clogging pizza and foamy beer, and I ended up clearing the plates of uneaten greens an hour later.

And with each scoop of ranch drizzled on the faux salad, it became clear that day and every day after: I hated faux facades. Say what you'll do and do what you'll say. If you want a greasy pizza, just eat it and love every bite. Own your choices. Any situation or person in my life should have the backstage match the front stage. Integrity is one and the same.

Tiny lessons of transformation like these appear throughout our lives. Little invitations that land at our feet. We just have to open the envelope and embrace the lesson within.

Today's message: I needed to follow my own advice. Exchange my well-crafted exterior of functional medicine idealism for practicality and vulnerability. I started by admitting I didn't have all the answers to running a seamless medical micropractice yet. But I was willing to listen to my community and address their needs. Using Google forms, I'd poll my patients often and listen to their feedback.

No one voluntarily signed up to learn about "Brain Health." But when the title was a tactile and compelling idea like "Sculpt Your Brain: How to Skip Your 2 p.m. Latte and Optimize Your Energy," it was suddenly irresistible. Soon, my audience of three grew into six. Then twelve. Then a full week of appointments.

Just imagine how easy motherhood could be if we used Google forms. As you're discharged home with your new baby in a swaddle, the nurses would teach you about swaddling and how to poll your children for feedback and actionable steps. "According to recent polling, 65 percent of the time, your baby prefers a gentle rocking at a tempo of forty beats per minute to initiate sleep compared to 23 percent who prefer singing." With Google forms, teens could communicate without speaking and a fresh report could be delivered to our maternal inbox every Monday morning. "Recent data suggests that the cause of your teen's argumentative mood is *not* the mandatory family picnic scheduled last Saturday, but the fact that the off-white Converse hi-tops were unavailable in their size."

Climbing into the role of a teacher/entertainer, I designed colorful handouts and worksheets. I revamped the slides to include polls and humorous memes. I binged on public speaking podcasts and hired a mentor. Audiences grew larger as I polished these lectures until the message became crystal clear: you are the author of your health destiny if you dare pick up the crayon. You paint your future, and I'm here to help mix the colors.

Soon my registration list went beyond the "friends and family" plan and filled with unrecognizable names of strangers I hadn't met. Our community was waking up to the possibility that our lives can be improved with targeted dietary and nutraceutical changes. People would stop me on the sidewalk with enthusiasm to report that their chronic sinusitis was resolved after eliminating dairy. Their insomnia evaporated once they started taking adaptogens to balance cortisol. Their hum of anxiety improved after they increased their intake of phytonutrients and omega-3 fatty acids. Lifelong diarrhea vanished with proper attention to probiotics and L-glutamine.

If simple changes could be this impactful, I couldn't stop here.

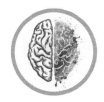

CHAPTER THIRTY-THREE

FENG SHUI FOR THE BODY

"But what if I just want to sell the whole house entirely?" the voice joked. I recognized her as the chai latte guest that wandered into my office a few weeks earlier. She had returned to my office as a workshop attendee and was learning how to "Build Your Ideal Functional Home."

I explained the concept, "Our body is a temple, but even temples need some upkeep. When you build a home, we don't expect the carpet to be in pristine condition five years later. We certainly don't expect the roof to never need replacing. Our bodies are the same way. This hour, we will be 'home inspectors' together and show you the areas in your body's 'home' that need some rehab after decades of wear and tear." Then I quipped, "Unfortunately we can't ask for a new body, but this will help give you direction on where to start your 'remodeling.' Give yourself a better *feng shui*, so to speak!"

Translating complex medical processes into relatable metaphors helps anchor understanding. Functional medicine organizes human physiology into several categories ("rooms"): hormonal, structural, energetic, toxic, immune, and gastrointestinal. I decided to use the home-building analogy to explain this complex process.

It starts with the soil. All homes are built on terrain that is unmodifiable. This soil represents antecedents—things we cannot change—like genetic inheritance (e.g., genetic risk for breast cancer or ApoE 4 Alzheimer's risk), DNA abnormalities (e.g., methylation issues that impact which genes are turned on or off), birth history (e.g., vaginal birth or C-section that affects our bacterial microbiome), past environmental exposure to toxins (e.g., living by a farm that sprays pesticides), and societal/cultural narratives (e.g., religious mandates that shape sense of self and community). While we cannot change the environment we build our home in, it's important to understand its characteristics.

Healthy homes need concrete foundations, which represents our gastrointestinal system. Our gastrointestinal tract is not just for food absorption and eventual elimination into the porcelain potty. It's responsible for 70 percent of our immune system[18] and can affect neurotransmitter production[19] that fuels our mood. Just like when there's a crack in a home's foundation, it becomes weaker, and likewise, this happens to our gastrointestinal tract in a variety of microscopic ways. Functional medicine calls these "triggers."

Years of proton-pump inhibitor[20] medication for acid reflux trigger intestinal permeability (leaky gut). Undiagnosed intestinal infections breach[21] the fortress of our gastrointestinal foundation. Endless examples of medications and diseases lead to disruption of gut tissues and promote intestinal permeability, also known as "leaky gut"[22].

Chronic disease develops when leaky gut is not addressed. The intestinal lining functions like the airport TSA security: they discern what items can pass their methodical scan safely and securely. The TSA determines: Do they need extra time to board? Do they have threatening firearms? Are they carrying infants and need extra assistance?

Unfortunately, things like chronic stress, surgery, exposure to environmental toxins, mold, viral and bacterial illnesses, trauma, and prescription medication can all cause the body's natural "TSA" scanning system to break down. Just like when TSA assumes everything is a threat—from eight-ounce shampoo bottles to tennis shoes—there's chaos and confusion at a deep, cellular level when your body's gastrointestinal system is vulnerable. Your body doesn't know what "threat" to respond to. Is this mold spore a problem? Will gluten cause brain fog? If unrecognized and not tended to, this miscommunication can result in an autoimmune disease[23] years later.

Once the concrete foundation has been poured, the second step of building any home is framing the supportive walls, as they need to be strong to hold our overall structure within. These walls represent our congruence of our external physical body with our internal emotional health. A well-aligned spine with musculoskeletal symmetry and healthy lymph flow is essential to a strong physique. Psychological balance is attained with regular thought work, awareness of boundaries, core values, and spiritual belonging. How we nurture our emotions directly impacts the health of our "home." For example, those who cling to unreleased anger are at higher risk of cardiac death[24]. Whereas those who practice expressing gratitude will show improved emotional regulation and well-being[25].

Once the walls are nailed in place, we turn our attention to the home's interior. Every Midwest home comes with a pre-installed argument button: a thermostat to balance the sweltering summers and frigid winters. Likewise, our body has intricate systems of cell signaling that maintain homeostasis. Imbalanced glucose and insulin will affect hormone and cortisol regulation as well as lipid abnormalities. Elevated levels of these inflammatory signals result in our "thermostat" working harder to maintain balance. We will continue to elevate our oxidative stress and inflammatory markers until our body breaks down and atherosclerosis, diabetes, obesity, and dementia results[26].

Unless you want to suffer the wrath of teenagers without Wi-Fi, all homes need electricity. The ideal "functional home" is energy efficient, and this comes from the powerhouses of our body: the mitochondria[27]. Our mitochondria are responsible for sensing our internal environment and alerting us to danger. When they get burdened with toxins or extra cortisol from chronic stress, these mitochondria can become inefficiently stuck[28]. We can suffer from increased infections, premature aging, and serious dysfunction. Since mitochondria reside mostly in brain and muscle, symptoms of mitochondrial inefficiency are brain fog, aching muscle pain, or overall fatigue.

The roof protects our body's temple and represents our overall immune system coordination. Evidence of poor immune maintenance is visible with skin changes (like eczema or hives), autoimmune disease (like lupus or rheumatoid arthritis), cancer, or ongoing gastrointestinal symptoms. Without a sturdy "roof," outside weather exposures like Electro-Motive Force (EMF)[29], herbicides/pesticides[30], heavy metals[31], and mold and chemical toxins[32] can seep in and affect our home's interior. Mitochondria will try to neutralize this danger, and this results in excessive amounts of oxidative stress[33].

This oxidative stress is like the smoke from our fireplace. It needs to be removed from our home safely. Our chimneys represent the main organs of detoxification: kidneys, liver, and our gastrointestinal tract. Their ability to eliminate this biochemical "exhaust" produced from high levels of oxidative stress[34] is crucial. Each of these organs can have challenges due to inherited alterations in biochemical pathways. If our "chimneys" aren't maintained and supported properly, we will have evidence of "ash and soot" in the form of free radicals and reactive oxygenation species[35] as our detoxification becomes sluggish. Fatty liver disease, renal failure, or constipation are common symptoms.

After this whirlwind home inspection tour, the class participants have a completed blueprint of areas requiring further attention. They're matched to one of the core food prescription plans from the Institute for Functional Medicine so they can support their vulnerabilities with targeted nutrition.

While this experience brought a fresh perspective on the power of nutrition, it underscored the complex relationship of tending to all areas in our body using a functional medicine perspective.

Moral of the workshop: if you're living in a home with beige linoleum floors, it's time for an update.

CHAPTER THIRTY-FOUR

WE ALL WANT IT

I opened my email and smiled:

I'm so thankful you left your conventional family medicine practice and branched out to do something different. This is an incredible service to our community. In a short time working with you, I lost twenty-five pounds, started sleeping through the night, and have more energy than I ever knew. I feel human again!!!

I marveled at the contrast from a year prior. My career memos didn't come from hospital administrators anymore. Instead, my feedback came directly from those who mattered most: my patients. No longer encumbered with layers of ancillary staff between us, I directly served them.

In my previous job as an employed family physician, I watched patients age, identified signs of disease, and carried out the standard screening recommendations. As the pace of the factory line quickened, it became harder to notice subtle nuances that might transform their health. Stepping aside to open a private practice in functional medicine allowed the space to investigate hidden biochemical imbalances, engage with emotional healing, and partner with patients at a deeper level with quicker results.

Comprehensive knowledge about a patient's unique physiology was within easy reach of rogue physicians like myself. Test kits from certified lab companies allowed patients to conveniently gather samples from home, giving us new data that was completely missed in a traditional setting. This gave hope for healing chronic diseases like rheumatoid arthritis, diabetes, and chronic fatigue. Working in concert with a primary care doctor to address emergent issues, functional providers can dampen inflammation, treat occult bacterial infections, remove excess toxins, and harmonize hormone levels to amplify wellness goals.

It felt a little bit like magic.

It was hard to believe that within a year, I had exchanged my humdrum job for daily play and wonder. I escaped my burnout and was single-handedly scaling a solo medical practice, teaching community workshops, producing colorful medical infographics, and speaking about applying a functional approach to modern medicine.

It was almost selfish to feel this good. But it'd be more selfish not to share.

I helped my local patients open new doorways of thinking and behaving. Now I needed to add the finishing touch that would bring us all together: creative flow state.

Adulthood puts most of us on a flow starvation diet. We neglect to make this part of our daily intake. Serving sizes of creativity shrink compared to childhood, where we exist in a supersized creative flow state most of our waking hours. Opportunities to experience flow state are everywhere[36].

Creative flow is how our brain *plays*—and it's addicting—a term called "autotelic." It generates feelings of happiness, well-being, and lowered stress. It also explains our decisions. We *crave* flow state. Just look at any recess playground across the nation, and you'll see team captains picking those most likely to guarantee achievement of flow state. Children will naturally avoid picking those of us, like me, who might thwart their basketball bliss with our clumsy limbs that aim at the opposing basket. (No matter, I would not choose them for my Pictionary tournament either.)

Unfortunately, we are all subconsciously on the search for flow in the wrong places. We scroll through social media. We binge on Netflix. When asked if we have a hobby, we wonder if "Sudoku" counts. Sadly, we don't make time to experience the joy of creative flow state.

Except there is one day that reminds us to get creative every year.

CHAPTER THIRTY-FIVE

BRACE YOURSELF

"What's this?" Emery asked as she opened the envelope. The return address came from the orthodontist in town. Our oldest, Owen, was to have his braces removed next week—coincidentally just as Emery would be enduring her first visit.

Casually placing forks into the dishwasher, I didn't respond. It was April 1st. I had been planning this feat for weeks. Tone and inflection were crucial in this moment. I didn't want to ruin it. That morning, I woke early to clutter the kitchen island with specifically positioned items, forcing her to occupy the only seat available: a single stool. A stool which happened to be placed directly in front of the hidden cell phone camera, recording every moment.

"I don't know." I shrugged.

Was my voice too shrill?

Emery unfolded the brochure as a gift card fell into her lap. "A gift card?" She continued reading the document, *"'We are excited to see you soon for your first orthodontic appointment. Please enjoy a milkshake to celebrate!'...Huh?"*

I stacked dishes and resisted the urge to survey the scene. The mention of milkshake had brought the rest of our children to the yard, and now Owen and Beckett are perched curiously around the island. Statute 288, section IV of the sibling rules dictated that unfair distribution of treats was immediate cause for mutiny.

"I don't get it," she uttered, turning over the tri-fold brochure in her hands, featuring bright photos of smiling teens with silver mouths. She continued, "*Our orthodontic office is proud to be the first to provide a real solution to the problem of metal bracket over-abundance...*'What? What is that? I don't understand."

Silence. More reading.

I felt the pressure of a chortle rising in my throat. Deep breath.

Owen peered over her shoulder as she persisted with confusion apparent on her brow, "*A trillion tons of used metal from orthodontic procedures sits in landfills across the United States*'... Wait. Huh?"

Owen plucked the brochure from her hands and continued reading with the snarky authority of an older brother, "*With our Sibling 2 Sibling program, we remove the metal brackets from one sibling and immediately reuse in another—*"

Emery blared, "WHAT?! No. EEEEEWWWWWWW!"

He resumed with renewed sadistic vigor, "Listen! It says: '*Using the latest HydroClenz technology, each bracket is sterilized before reuse. Minor bacterial contamination is treated with our patented Black Tar Gargle*'... You're getting *my* braces!!!!!" He threw a valiant fist in the air.

Horror landed on her face in full force. She whipped her head around. "WHAT? NO...no. For real? MOM?" She scanned my face for hope.

I swallowed so hard, I could feel the chortle lodged painfully in my throat.

Feigning innocence, I reached for the brochure and continued reciting the testimonials I had carefully typed days earlier, "Now just hold on, Emery. This is a considerably big discount, and it sounds like a great opportunity: '*A fantastic brother-and-sister bonding experience! My daughter was relieved she didn't taste her brother's saliva! It feels good knowing I'm saving money AND the environment!*'"

CJ gave the rehearsed final approval as the fatherly voice of financial reason chimed in, "That will save us a lot of money."

Her lower lip trembled as Owen bellowed into the air: "*My* braces are coming off next week and GOING INTO *YOUR* MOUTH!"

Her eyes darted around the room. "Ew! No way. Is this for real? No, please. That's gross. I just *know* they won't clean it."

I felt her panic. I couldn't stand another moment and shouted, "APRIL FOOLS!"

Relief spread across her face as disappointment settled on Owen's.

I read somewhere that humans experience more pleasure at the alleviation of pain or discomfort, rather than during a happy moment itself. In reality, motherhood can be a long game of discomfort, too. I place reliability and integrity at the top of my predictable agenda of motherhood. This means, while I'll always be punctual to dance class, I'll also admit when I went ten miles over the speed limit to get there. My kids can trust me 364 days of the year.

April Fools' Day is the jolt of novelty and surprise that keeps kids on their toes by reminding them how creative their mother can be.

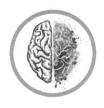

CHAPTER THIRTY-SIX

MITOCHONDRIA

"But I'm a *horrible* artist!" complained my first patient of the day. "I've never had to bring a drawing to my first medical appointment before."

She pointed toward the sketch in her hand, referring to her first "homework" assignment.

"There's no such thing as *bad art*!" I exclaimed. "Look at your masterpiece! It's so expressive! Can you please give me a tour?"

She drew herself with hiking boots on the edge of a canyon (she admitted that she hadn't been able to hike very far without significant joint pain in the last year). Sprouting from her back were feathery wings (she wants to learn how to say "no" and flee from the burden of stress). Large, funky sunglasses adorned her face, and her mouth was a wide, crescent grin. A gardening trowel was in her left hand, and a needle and thread in her right. (She had stopped her favorite hobbies of landscaping and cross-stitching years ago when fatigue dampened her mood.) She drew electric bolts coming out of her crown (to signify her improved cognitive thinking and concentration). Finally, a collection of teeny, tiny toilets were visible on the horizon.

"What's this? Are you vacationing in Kohler, Wisconsin?" I referenced the famous plumbing company by the same name.

"Nope." She giggled. "The toilets represent my goal to be *far away* from a bathroom because I finally have control over my—um, *elimination.*" She blushed.

Through a series of tests, we discovered inefficient mito-chondrial function and an undiagnosed *Prevotella* bacterial overgrowth in her intestines, which could have triggered her genetic predisposition for rheumatoid arthritis. Once she finished the gut-healing protocol, rebalanced her gut microbiome, and supported her mitochondria properly, her fatigue evaporated. Her joint pains were gone, and she was counting sheep in her sleep and no longer counting toilets.

"I feel like a teenager again!" she exclaimed. "How is this happening?"

"It's your mitochondria," I explained. "They're like actual microscopic teenagers in your body. They can be finicky and sensitive. And just like teens, they require lots of sleep and quality food. If you stay up all night, or don't sleep well, you'll literally feel them in every cell of your body. They're what caused your achy pain, brain fog, and drained energy."

These mighty mitochondria—the "energy powerhouses" live all over your body, but your brain and muscles need them the most[37]. Just like budding teenagers, mitochondria want independence, but can't quite take care of themselves. And they're a bit judgmental. It's part of survival; they're constantly surveying their environment[38], deciding which crowd they fit in, and choosing whether they need to freeze, fight, or flee[39]. If they've had restful sleep and wholesome food, they have great potential to be energetic, bubbly, and exuberant. They might even give a hug, share a seat at their cafeteria table, or pick up a dirty sock.

But when these "teenagers" are sleep-deprived and slurping down processed foods like ramen noodles and Mountain Dew, they'll crash with irritability and inflammation. They'll sequester themselves in their rooms and release their toxicity in the form of reactive oxygen species[40]. They shrink in size and express their anger by discharging their oxidized DNA, causing us to feel prematurely old and shortening our life span[41, 42].

Thankfully, we're renewing our supply of inner "teenagers" constantly[43], making newer mitochondrial generations based on our immediate needs. Slothing it out during a weekend marathon of eighties horror films? Our mitochondria will respond by down-regulating their efficiency and quality. Training for a marathon? Our mitochondria will rise to our aid, becoming denser, more efficient, and crowded in number.

If we feed them proper nutrient-dense foods[44] that contain all their favorites like alpha-lipoic acid, L-carnitine, B vitamins, and antioxidants, we'll directly feel their glow every day. We'll be able to think clearer (thanks to increased[45] brain derived neurotrophic factor (BDNF)—it's like "growth hormone" for the brain) and feel stronger and happier. Neuroplasticity (the ability to make new, faster, and more efficient connections in our brain) flourishes with healthy mitochondria fertilized by BDNF.

I nodded to the newly refurbished patient in front of me and concluded, "You started by taking care of the foundation of your functional home: your gastrointestinal tract. Once we balanced your internal ecosystem of bacteria and eradicated your yeast overgrowth, your body was able to process food properly again. We also identified mitochondrial insufficiencies on functional testing. Instead of reaching for a muffin or granola bar, you've been creating smoothies with mitochondria-rich foods like kale, avocado, and strawberries. You started supplementing with medical-grade carnitine, alpha-lipoic acid, CoQ10, B vitamins, and antioxidants. Your moods lifted[46] and now your brain is relishing the new neuroplastic connections[47]!"

I continued to explain that despite all the proper fortification, mitochondria—like teenagers—still need some protection from the caustic outside world. They're not impervious to toxic influences.

"After we talked about the damage that glyphosate does to your mitochondria[48], you wrestled the bottle of RoundUp from your husband (since chronic exposure[49] to glyphosate leads to dysfunctional mitochondria) and threw out all your teflon cooking supplies that contain chemicals[50] that poison your cells. You also replaced all your plastics with BPA-free options and only chose lotions without PABA or phthalates[51]. All of these help keep your biochemistry in great shape."

Putting a few simple habits in place helped her mitochondria "teenagers" get off the couch and start participating in life again. The most impactful was intermittent fasting (time-restricted feeding)[52]. Our bodies don't do well snacking all day long from abundant food choices available. We end up storing more adipose and increase our risk of glucose dysregulation and chronic disease.

Timing is everything. When we have an empty tank for at least twelve hours during every twenty-four-hour period, our mitochondria are triggered to "clean their rooms" and remove that rusty oxidative stress from our cells that causes premature aging[53]. If feeding is compressed further into a smaller window of eight hours, the effects are even better: your mitochondria will hum with energy[54]! They'll coax better neuroplasticity[55] and dampen inflammation[56] throughout your body.

"So you're saying that these mitochondria teens are powerful. They light up our bodies like glow sticks at a rave?" she summarized.

"Minus the ecstasy," I confirmed.

CHAPTER THIRTY-SEVEN
INTEGRATE

"I am not sure I can do that," he said. Mr. Stanford was my third patient that week who dismissed my suggestion of regular meditation. "I'm very high strung. I won't have the patience because I'm just not wired that way. I can't force myself to just *sit* and be *still*. My job requires me to be prolific at all times."

I nodded solemnly. Namaste, dude. The type A light in me sees the Type A light in you. I began my negotiations.

"Space and silence is essential to the creativity recipe. Integrating your brain hemispheres helps you optimize your ability to regulate emotion and lower stress. I promise you: anyone can do this. It gets easier the more you practice. Let me tell you about a patient I had years ago. If he can do it, so can you."

It was Monday morning, and my first patient arrived early to his 8 a.m. appointment. As our staff reported to the clinic, they noticed a single, rusted gold Sedan parked in the lot. He was calmly waiting. Inside the building, computers whirred to life, overhead lights snapped on. The moment the entrance door was unlocked at 8:01 a.m., he marched swiftly into the waiting room.

His chart landed on my desk. I picked it up, flipped open to the office note and paused. I read it twice and looked at my nurse for confirmation.

"What?" I asked my nurse as I scrutinized his chart. "That can't possibly be real. It says, *insect trapped in ear*?!" She nodded incredulously.

I opened the door to exam two and surveyed the scene.

Perched upright was Mr. Henrickson, a gentleman, approximately mid-forties. Wearing his neatly pressed security officer uniform, he stared straight ahead without acknowledging my entrance. He remained rigid and unwavering as I walked directly into his line of sight and offered my hand to greet him. He pumped it deliberately.

"So it says here that you have an *insect trapped in your ear?*" I asked.

"Yes ma'am," he responded.

"But...you've had it...*since Saturday evening?*" I paused. "It's Monday. That's nearly thirty-six hours. Are you sure it's an insect?"

"Yes ma'am. My wife and I are temporarily living in one of our in-law's trailers until we close on our house next week. It's overrun with cockroaches. We thought we'd gotten most of them before moving in." He flinched involuntarily and continued, "That is, until we went to bed Saturday night. I felt something crawl in my ear and immediately turned on the light to tell my wife."

I shuddered reflexively.

"My wife is a nurse, so she went to get her old otoscope from nursing school. She looked in and saw this tiny cockroach. We spent all of Sunday trying to figure out a way to get it out. First, I would wait with the lights off. When I could feel the little bugger move, I'd tell my wife to get the tweezers. But every time she shined her light, it would turn around and scurry deeper into my ear. I swear I could feel it scratching all weekend. The nearest ER is over an hour away, and roads were horrible, so I learned how to take deep breaths and meditate by watching a video. I did this whenever I felt the scratching again. All weekend long. Scratching and breathing. Scratching and breathing. And now here I am."

I could barely control my grimace, but duty called. I pulled his ear and peeked inside with my otoscope to find exactly the monstrous image he described: a tiny cockroach scratching on his tympanic membrane. I yelped.

My nurse returned with the antidote: a syringe filled with lidocaine. I saturated his ear canal with the solution until the evil adversary was dead. I removed him with forceps, bit by bit. A real-life game of Operation without the glowing red nose buzzer.

A few minutes later, Mr. Henrickson was the proud owner of the cleanest ear in Missouri and my trash can held remnants of a tattered entomology exhibit: thorax, antennae, abdomen, wing.

I summarized to the patient in front of me, "If *this man* can learn to breathe and be patiently zen all weekend, *anyone* can learn to meditate. He probably didn't realize his crash course in meditation was lowering stress cortisol[57] with each mindful breath. It allowed him to disconnect from his reactivity to that insect stimuli. Even when you are just getting started with meditation[58], you weaken this neural sensitivity, so when you experience upsetting sensations, you can more easily look at them rationally."

As Light Watkins says in his book *Bliss More: How to Succeed at Meditation without Trying*, "It's been suggested that of the tens of thousands of thoughts we supposedly have each day, we recycle as many as 90 percent of them from yesterday. Assuming that's true, then our monkey mind is more or less swinging toward the same recycled thoughts, and processing the same recycled information, with the same frequency, in the same way, day after day after day after day. Without some intervention like meditation, the way you felt about your life yesterday is probably how you will feel about it today, tomorrow, and the next day."

I nodded again to the patient in front of me. "You mentioned feeling lackluster and dull. You also said you 'never have time' and feel like you're 'always stressed.' When our thoughts rehearse the same script every day, we can get stuck in a rut. Perhaps it's time to learn how to launder those recycled thoughts. Integrating your brain hemispheres will help you with this. If you want to help balance your cortisol and be more prolific at work, you'll experience more creative inspiration if you meditate daily[59]. Your brain will get out of the stodgy, analytical beta waves in the prefrontal cortex and activate your colorful, default creative network."

Mr. Stanford seemed unconvinced. I continued my pledge.

"Functional medicine is less about cultivating harmony in your physiology. And meditation has been scientifically proven to help improve[60] concentration levels and increase[61] your working memory capacity, focus, and attention span. Meditation is an excellent[62] tool in increasing right- and left-brain harmony. A 2015 study[63] from the *Journal of the American Medical Association* found that mindfulness meditation alleviates depression symptoms and daytime fatigue." I typed a few tutorial smartphone apps and book suggestions into his visit summary.

"Meditation is like squeezing out your brain sponge so you can fill it up again with better thoughts. It's the negative white space of an artist's canvas. Sure, it takes a bit of practice, but I promise you, even just seven minutes a day will change your brain," I concluded.

"Well, Doc, seven minutes in heaven sure has a different meaning compared to when I was a teen," Mr. Stanford joked.

Months later, he graduated from my services with renewed vigor. After we discovered he had low testosterone levels, they were corrected with appropriate nutraceuticals like stinging nettles[64] and grape seed extract. Adaptogens like ashwagandha[65] lowered his high cortisol levels and provided deeper sleep.

He reported that he was able to conduct his executive meetings with more enthusiasm and flair, and his moodiness had stabilized at home as well. "When our dog chewed my favorite shoes, I didn't fly off the handle." His sleep felt restful, and he even started playing golf again.

"Once I gave meditation a try, I noticed my thought rodeo slowed down, and I had more energy at the same time. But most of all, I'll never think of cockroaches the same again."

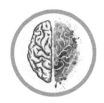

CHAPTER THIRTY-EIGHT

NOTICE

"Creativity isn't just about innovating or making art—it's about living creatively. We can approach any situation in life with a creative spirit. We all can dream, explore, discover, build, ask questions, and seek answers—to be creators. Creative self-expression opens us up to who we are and invites us to explore and express our own unique set of qualities and experiences, to play with ambiguities, and to connect the dots in a way that they've never been connected before."

—Scott Barry Kaufmann, *Wired to Create*

Pattern recognition is essential to sparking a creative epiphany.

"You know what? Finding a job will be *super* easy for me," Emery remarked at the kitchen island. "Teacher, doctor, janitor, carnival worker—I've ruled out lots of jobs already."

"How's that?" I asked.

She shrugged. "Because I hate puke so much."

Kids are experts at connecting the dots. Adults? Not so much. So I started underscoring the importance of inward-focused attention in my delivery of medical care. I called on my patients to feel their body's symptoms. Without proper attunement, it's like driving a car without noticing the faulty "check engine" light. For years, many patients were dismissed by doctors telling them,

"Everything is normal. You're *fine,*" furthering their perception that their body could not be trusted.

I started with somatic awareness. The Medical Symptoms Questionnaire[66] is a useful method in functional medicine to calculate a numerical score on overall symptoms. A score of less than twenty is normal for the expected aches and pains in a walking meat skeleton. Higher scores commonly indicated more symptom awareness, but could also imply a bad day. Subjective measurements are best paired with objective data.

While we waited for results of functional testing to identify the internal specifics on hormones, vitamins, or other information, I tended to their supportive "walls." I'd encourage patients to notice their inner emotional environment, thought patterns, and energy drains to see if there were connections to their overall wellness. Is it a coincidence that you have a migraine every Tuesday night after your weekly meeting with that oppositional client? Perhaps your bloated, sour stomach on Saturday mornings is due to the Friday fish fry the night before. Clarity is possible if we schedule our own personal State of the Union to reflect on habitual patterns.

"You want me to do this *during* a business meeting?" Mrs. Taylor asked. She was halfway through her program to rebalance her menopausal hormones we discovered on testing. A fearless CEO, she knew how to settle disputes, make life-changing decisions, and elevate her company's economic growth. But menopause had left her with restless sleep, daily anxiety, and uncertainty. She had significantly elevated cortisol, a stress hormone, that was worsened by her nightly brandy Old Fashioned and bowl of gelato.

Mrs. Taylor could handle it all; as a working mom of four, she routinely juggled her executive responsibilities with soccer games, community fundraisers, and science fairs. She had lost her energy autonomy somewhere along the way and needed to create better emotional boundaries in the walls of her home's "blueprint."

"With practice, you can access your intuition by performing a body scan," I explained. "The next time you're feeling uncertain about any decision, try checking in with yourself. Where do you feel the thoughts in your body? Are they pleasantly nudging you forward? Or are they feeling cautious and sore in your body elsewhere? Often we say *yes* to an overabundance of commitments, neglecting our own unspoken desires and wants. By checking in with our body's wisdom, this might help you use the Two-Word Miracle cure: *for me.*"

I continued, "When those tiny words *for me* are added at the end of a sentence, it solves all conflict without judgment. It helps you practice building those boundaries again. Let's try it: 'Thank you for the invitation to the Mega Baller Charity Gala for Super Dope Schools Everywhere. But that long-term commitment doesn't work *for me.*'"

Journaling helped to solidify reference points and create a historical log of progress. When Mrs. Taylor paired this inward-focused attention with supplements to correct hormonal imbalance like Indole-3-Carbinol (I3C) from brassica vegetables[67], and diindolylmethane (DIM) from cruciferous vegetables[68], she emerged a few months later to exclaim, "My moods are more in check now, and I haven't had this kind of well-being in years! This really worked—*for me!*" She winked.

CHAPTER THIRTY-NINE
DIVERGENT

"Where's the purple marker?!" the resident doctor demanded.

The group of newly minted physicians were huddled together on the floor, coloring their own pictures. We were an hour into my "Prescribing Creativity" workshop, outlining the long-term benefits of applying daily flow state. We had just learned how creativity requires a flexibility of convergent and divergent thinking[69], and they were engrossed in this new activity.

I quoted Dr. Shelley Carson, a Harvard PhD psychologist, saying, "Creativity is a brain activation pattern that can be amplified with a little effort and a bit of practice."

We can't manifest these feats of ingenuity if our brains aren't primed and ready.

"I'm a doctor turned drug dealer." I quipped to the crowd. "Creativity is my drug of choice. Why not? Flow state is the only time our brain produces all five happy neurochemicals[70] of dopamine, norepinephrine, serotonin, anandamide, and endorphins. And I am here to get you hooked on it, and then teach you how to cook it up on your own—like every good drug dealer would."

Creative flow state is the only drug that gets you 'high' faster with each time you use it. And the effects last long after the activity ceases[71]. If we capitalize on our innate ability to think expansively, we can effectively get ourselves out of any mess. However, creativity needs the right conditions to express itself.

If your amygdala (the fear center of your brain) is chronically activated, it will sabotage your ability to think clearly or generate new ideas.

To wake up their divergent thoughts, I started with a doodle from the famous Torrance Creativity Test. Created by Ellis Paul Torrance, the Torrance Tests of Creative Thinking (TTCT) includes simple tests of abstract thinking and other problem-solving skills. The residents were challenged to come up with possible solutions to complete a drawing. When you play with this flexibility of thought, these skills can be transferable to find solutions elsewhere in life.

Usually there's one oppositional participant in the room, uncertain to comply with the frivolity of play. They haven't reconnected with their creative muse yet. I subconsciously nickname them the "Purple Marker Person," because in the end, they're usually the one demanding the purple marker to complete their arduous masterpiece.

As burnout is rampant in the medical profession, studies show art can help[72] doctors release uncomfortable emotions and improve empathy. When physicians were trained to achieve flow[73] state by understanding their signature strengths and maximizing time spent on challenging tasks that match one's strengths (as opposed to spending time on activities that are less appropriate for one's skill set) their work felt effortless, well-being rose, and patients had better outcomes.

"Dude, my picture looks *lame*," the purple marker resident declared. "And I don't see how this relates to my being a physician. Our jobs are dictated by evidence-based, scientific research and logic."

"Ah yes, but who comes up with ideas that become standard of care?" I responded. "Being a physician is the ultimate in creativity! What other career requires you to use all your senses? You watch your patient's body language to notice they walk with a left limp from a psoas muscle spasm. You palpate their abdomen to find a hardened liver edge that might indicate cirrhosis. You listen to the tone and inflection of their voice as you interpret their mood after a recent job loss. Then, you use your analytical skills together with your perceptive skills to weave a tapestry of their past and present to plan for a new future. That's amazingly creative!"

There is an art to medicine as much as there is a science. As our profession has imposed greater value on data collection and metrics over the authenticity of human touch, we've planted the seeds for dissatisfaction and burnout.

"As I helped patients address chronic trauma and stress in my office, I realized that young medical students and physicians could benefit from similar help. If we wait until we're burned out, we're unlikely to reach our full potential. We need to learn how to get out of our own way," I explained. "It starts with sleep. The right brain hemisphere is consistently the more active side during sleep. It's your right brain that handles 'housekeeping' duties while[74] sleeping. While the left side of your brain takes some time off to relax, the right side gets busy dumping files from your hippocampus, pushing information into long-term storage, and organizing your memories from the day."

If we aren't following a robust sleep/wake routine, we aren't going to manifest innovative divergent solutions because our brains get full and cluttered with extraneous, fragmented information. Many great artists have said[75] that they do their best work either very early in the morning or late at night. Vladimir Nabokov, the prolific Russian novelist, started writing immediately after he woke up at 6 or 7 a.m. Benjamin Franklin coined the phrase, "Early to bed, early to rise makes a man healthy, wealthy, and wise." Frank Lloyd Wright made a practice of waking up at 3 or 4 a.m. and working for several hours before heading back to bed[76]. No matter when it is, individuals with high creative output will often figure out what time it is that their minds fire up, and structure their days around this.

Resilient neuroplasticity is essential for a rigorous medical career. When we sign up for a degree in medicine, we gain a front-row ticket to witness the extremes of all human conditions from the joys of birth to the tragedy of death. Though we might feel equipped to guide others through painful diagnoses and treatments, it will never prepare us for personal adversity. Being a doctor doesn't mean you "get out of jail free," nor does it save you from infertility, motor vehicle accidents, alcoholism, depression, SIDS, cancer, divorce, or suicide.

Your hard work results in a medical degree, but doesn't guarantee you can stop hemorrhages from pouring onto your eighties linoleum floor or avoid the heartache of burnout. This chronic trauma burns our delicate neurons into overdone crisps, incapable of resiliency or empathy. We need to protect ourselves through nourishing our mind and spirit.

The residents shared their artistry. Pride flickered across their weary, post-call faces. The same doodle was incorporated into a dozen different drawings as it was transformed into flowers, flags, profiles, animals, buildings. Evidence we are still brilliantly curious and creative at our core, no matter how tired. I prepared to close our session with some final thoughts.

"The moment we admit to someone else that we're a physician, they know all about us. In those three words, others can accurately assume our work ethic, core values, and ability to delay gratification. They can reliably predict our high school GPA and anemic social calendar. As we conclude our workshop today, I want you to ask yourself, 'What makes me *interesting*?' Being a doctor shouldn't be the *only* intriguing part of your life." My voice escalated. "What *else* makes your eyes glow when you talk about it? If you could devote 10,000 hours to instantly become a master at something, what would that be? What are *you* passionate about? Creativity is exactly what makes us come alive. Make it a priority to explore what makes you curious every day and keep coloring outside the lines."

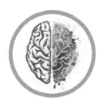

CHAPTER FORTY

ASHES TO ASHES

"It's kinda like running a four-minute mile after Bannister proved it's possible," remarked my colleague, a fellow physician. I was mentoring her to build her own creative micropractice. We were online in a Zoom meeting room, discussing ways to engage and empower her rural town hundreds of miles away. It felt pleasantly reminiscent: like passing a virtual plate of cookies to my neighbor in this growing legion of functional medicine practitioners.

The inspiration of the human spirit is contagious. Experts previously believed it was impossible to run a four-minute mile, until Roger Bannister[77] proved them wrong by running a mile in 3:59:4 in May of 1954. After he obliterated this limiting belief, the door opened for other runners to achieve this milestone. Similarly, runners who finished races from 5K to full marathons have increased[78] from five million participants in 1990 to 19 million participants in 2013.

Physicians are a gritty, self-determined bunch. We are the marathon runners of healthcare. We signed up for this challenge, oftentimes starting in high school. We run interval sprints. We run hills. We stretch. We anticipate and plan. We don't complain. All because we are promised that "someday" we will reach a comfortable pace and stride that feels effortless. We carb load until our muscles ache. And yet each lap gets faster and faster.

We skimp on sleep and shorten our recovery time, just to get up and lace up our shoes and don our white coat for another day.

There's no medal at our finish line, because there *is no finish line*. Physicians sign up for the race that lasts a lifetime. We barely sense the pace quickening and the incline steepening. With no end in sight, we suffer in silence as over 400 medical professionals die by suicide[79] annually. Now that "burnout" has been deemed as an achievable diagnosis (ICD-10: Z73.0), it has opened up the conversation to view this as what it truly is: an epidemic of disconnection. Of dissociation. Discontent. Disillusionment. Complete castration of our ability to be unique healers due to our lack of autonomy[80] to judge our own pace and run our own race.

The medical career marathon we were promised differs greatly from what we're running. Lap after lap, we slowly realize the enormity of this heartbreak: there is no opportunity for individuality. We must step in line with the predetermined pace despite the cost to mind and body. As doctors leave the profession, retire early, or avoid signing on for this "marathon" entirely, the United States will see a shortage[81] of up to nearly 122,000 physicians by 2032 according to new data published today by the AAMC (Association of American Medical Colleges).

Our medical profession has plenty of our own Roger Bannisters, just like my colleague on Zoom: fellow physicians that resigned from their employed settings and dared to create a world they want to live in. Finally, my pathologic organizational skills and addiction to list-making came in handy. In our hour together, I organized her thoughts into actionable next steps so she could incorporate shared group medical visits in her practice. This shared Google document became her personal roadmap to sovereignty.

"You're ahead of the game. The future of medicine can't be contained within the four walls of a tiny exam room any longer. Branching into shared group medical visits will be the only way to reach the growing masses," I explained. "Cleveland Clinic has been hosting shared medical appointments[82] with great success. In addition to educating others about their chronic disease, it alleviates their feeling of loneliness[83]. Sitting alongside others in the community with similar struggles helps instill courage to try new recipes, exercises, and habits."

The more I worked with practitioners to help them build their own micropractice, it underscored the need to support our underappreciated creativity. As our population continues to suffer with the increasing burden of chronic disease, we will need to rely on our collective innovation to deliver impactful and sustainable healthcare. But it will take the utmost in creativity to make it happen, or else we suffer the same burnout seeping into the groundwater of historical healthcare.

I concluded our visit and reflected on the burned-out pawns in healthcare. The medical students. The residents. The physicians.

I felt this unrelenting pang. I wanted to send a "love letter" to all of them because I understood their collective distress. If I could help my colleagues with one act, it would be to awaken the gift of creativity within them—it's the ultimate wild card that can win at any hand.

This love letter would start by demonstrating how stress can cause intestinal permeability and proper attention to mitochondria can help. There would be convergent and divergent activities to increase thought flexibility. I'd include organizational tips to help increase work efficiency and colorful infographics to make teaching fun again. There would be guidance on accessing flow state, so participants can benefit from this happy neurochemical release. I'd bring out the kindergartener in everyone with colorful hands-on projects using household items within reach. Finally, I'd supply a printable workbook with delicious recipes and activities that integrate their brain hemispheres to promote neuroplasticity.

The power of creativity can be accessed in the blink of an eye and within each breath. To many, the thought of "practicing" breathing seems as outlandish as practicing creativity. Yet, learning simple breathing techniques can affect well-being, stress[84], and vagal tone (the part of the autonomic nervous system responsible for "rest and digest"). Altering breathing patterns can improve mood and sleep[85].

The solitary goal of my "love letter" would be to recognize that creativity is just as important. Creativity is as essential as oxygen, carbon, or broccoli. It's worthy of daily practice.

And Right Brain Rescue[86] was born.

CHAPTER FORTY-ONE
THE SIXTH VITAL SIGN

Right Brain Rescue was more than an online resource about proper stress management and burnout avoidance. It became a reminder to reflect on the congruence between healthcare and provider. A beacon of colorful sparkle to defy the monotonous slog. Most of all, Right Brain Rescue was a triumphant call to action, begging us to dig deep and sculpt our one masterpiece that is life.

"Some of us believe that if we could only find the perfect job or work for the right company, many of our issues related to lack of fulfillment or occupational frustration would vanish. (Many) consider leaving their job to find something that's a better fit. While there's nothing wrong with seeking work that's fulfilling and that matches our personal skills and goals, often these conversations are less about the job itself and more about unrealistic expectations toward the employer or an overall lack of self-knowledge. Upon leaving their job, many workers find that they are right back in a place of dissatisfaction within a matter of months after taking a new one.

"Why does this happen so frequently to the best and brightest among us? The problem is that many of us spend a lot of time thinking about what we want to do but little time thinking about who we really are."

—Todd Henry, *The Accidental Creative*

Temperature, pulse, blood pressure, and respiratory rate.

These are vital signs. They measure your *vitality*. Every time you sit in a doctor's exam room, two things are guaranteed. First, there's never a clock within sight. Second, vital signs will be measured.

In 2001, Pain was introduced as the fifth vital sign[87] by the Joint Commission after discovering that physicians were "undertreating pain" according to patient feedback. Adding this as a routine vital sign would ensure that pain was a topic discussed at every visit.

Posters with various cartoon faces started popping up in exam rooms. As the expectations included in a medical visit mounted, nurses were under the clock to finish all their tasks within their check-in process. In between the sounds of Velcro ripping from the blood pressure cuff and the beeping of an ear thermometer, patients would be pressured to urgently point to a face representing their relative ease or discomfort. This was very confusing to doctor and patient alike, since pain doesn't keep you *alive* at all...so how was this a *vital* sign?

This blemish in our medical history timeline marks the instant when doctors were unrealistically expected to "fix" every patient on their conveyor belt in fifteen minutes or less with this newly updated set of "vital signs."

Even Buddha agrees that pain is inevitable and suffering is optional. What you focus on, grows, and what you think, you become. Therefore, we shouldn't be surprised that we are experiencing an opioid crisis decades after we planted the negative seeds of confirmation bias. Now doctors and patients are suffering the consequences. Healthcare is intended to support *health*. Instead, we have a toxic system that is decaying, bringing the most vibrant minds down with it.

Our true adversary in this short life is burnout: *emotional exhaustion, depersonalization, and low perceived personal achievement*. From education to farming, military to police, burnout grows in all our industries. If we're not vigilant, burnout creeps into our relationships, our bodies, our bedrooms, and our parenting.

Burnout wouldn't stand a chance if we proactively supported our brains by nurturing neuroplasticity in our healers, teaching them the soothing and therapeutic ways to tap into flow state. We could become more nimble to observe changes in our environment, notice internal shifts in values, and recognize alternative paths before our essence rots on the vine.

When "pain" was made the fifth vital sign, we were rewarded with twenty years of depression, burnout, and drug addiction. Having "pain" as the last item assessed in our vital sign measurement prompted patients to focus on negativity. Imagine what could happen if we conclude our vital sign measurement and ask about creativity. What if we asked our patients what makes them come alive, what fuels their spark? Instead, patients would reflect on joy, curiosity, fulfillment, and awe.

"Creativity is important for remaining healthy, remaining connected to yourself and connected to the world," says Christianne Strang[88], a professor of neuroscience at the University of Alabama Birmingham and the former president of the American Art Therapy Association[89].

Instead of concluding our vital sign measurement by concentrating on pain, what if we reflected on what makes us come *alive*? Maybe in twenty years, we would generate a renaissance of innovative healers and empowered patients instead of chronic depression and opioid addiction. Creativity is essential to awakening humanity's purpose: to elevate and evolve our place in this universe.

Creativity is the sixth vital sign we need.

CHAPTER FORTY-TWO

WORDS

"Mom? What's your favorite word?" Beckett asked during another typical day of Muber duty.

"Hm. That's a very interesting question. I haven't thought much about it," I conceded.

"My favorite word is *colonoscopy*. Try it. Just say: COH-lohn-AHH-scoh-pee. It's so fun to say," he remarked emphatically. I burst out laughing.

"I suppose it is. Kinda like an exercise for your tongue." I snickered, incapable of keeping a straight face, but loving his ingenuity all at once.

The audacious truth is the world is crumbling around us. Burnout is seeping into the groundwater, and we need all brains on deck to find solutions. We need vibrant, colorful, sparkly thinking that approaches problems with playful curiosity. The only way to do this is to exercise our creativity, starting with you, dear reader.

Practicing the sixth vital sign of creativity daily is less about following an exact method or protocol, but instead using the tools to carve your own canyon. Perhaps this book inspires you to dust off those knitting needles or explore a new hobby. Maybe you'll think differently about what's at the end of your fork. Or you'll sense your tectonic core values shifting underneath and approach changes with open-ended awareness. I hope at the very least, you'll put creativity back into daily rotation and be more discerning on how you spend your precious brain energy on those projects and people that help you bloom.

Who knows, maybe this will be kindling to a creative fire that will upend a solution to climate destruction, racial inequality, patriarchy, or the end to world hunger. I'm secretly hoping for a new terrycloth material that withstands mildew, no matter how long it's crumpled on a teen's bathroom floor. And if you're yearning for more practice, maybe you'll visit Right Brain Rescue[90] to thwart burnout by learning steps to properly fuel your physiology, heal your gut, and enhance cognitive flexibility.

"When the artist is alive in any person, whatever his kind of work may be, he becomes an inventive, searching, daring, self-expressive creature. He becomes interesting to other people. He disturbs, upsets, enlightens, and opens ways for better understanding. Where those who are not artists are trying to close the book, he opens it and shows there are still more pages possible."

—American painter, Robert Henri

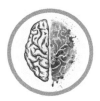

CHAPTER FORTY-THREE

LINES

I was nine years old, standing in the funeral home again. I ran my fingers along the brass handle of the casket, tracing the cold lines of mortality.

"Mom—what's this?" I pointed to a protruding cap embedded on the corner of the coffin.

She paused with curling iron in hand, steam rising up from the deceased's white hair.

"That's an identification capsule," she replied matter-of-factly, then resumed wielding her hot iron with a sizzle. "If the casket is disentombed, that tube stays intact. It makes it easier to recognize who is inside. It has all the important details like name, birth date, life stats, et cetera." My mother's fingers carefully separated the snowy satin locks. Sizzle, click, sizzle.

I tapped on the shiny end cap with my fingernail. I ponder what was handwritten on all the scrolls buried deep beneath the topsoil. If we're lucky, we get to accumulate a multitude of events between our birth and death dates. These unknown dates force a finite length to our invisible scroll.

What titles will fill the space on our scrolls? Mother, father, doctor, sister, coworker, wife, partner, lover, friend, volunteer? But what about vomit cleaner, Muber driver, napkin origami folder, ninja gift-giver, party hoster, off-key singer?

Who deems a title worthy of mention?

Who decides what is finalized on this tiny parchment?

It's certainly not large enough to hold our most meaningful memories. So who draws the line when the original line artist is lying six feet below the tulips?

In the end, it doesn't matter who decides what's written on these superficial lines.

We are all unbreakably permanent. Made of the same magnificent, neverending chains of carbon and magic, oxygen and sparkle—our lines extending infinitely in both directions.

Besides, lines only exist so we can color outside them.

REFERENCES

1. Erstling, T. (n.d.) The Neurochemistry of Flow States. Retrieved from https://troyerstling.com/the-neurochemistry-of-flow-states/

2. Arkowitz, H., Lilienfeld S.O. (2012 August, 1). EMDR: Taking a Closer Look. Retrieved from: https://www.scientificamerican.com/article/emdr-taking-a-closer-look/

3. Eye Movement Desensitization and Reprocessing (EMDR) Therapy. (2017, May). Retrieved from: https://www.apa.org/ptsd-guideline/treatments/eye-movement-reprocessing

4. Jenkins, S. (2014, May 6). EMDR Therapy: Separating Fact from Fiction. Retrieved from: https://www.goodtherapy.org/blog/emdr-therapy-separating-fact-from-fiction-0506144

5. Danylchuk, L. (2015, September 1). What Do EMDR, Running, and Drumming Have in Common? Retrieved from: https://www.goodtherapy.org/blog/what-do-emdr-running-and-drumming-have-in-common-0901154

6. Drybye, L. N., Shanafelt, T.D., Gill, P.R., Satele, D.V., & West, C.P. (2019). Effect of a Professional Coaching Intervention on the Well-being and Distress of Physicians: A Pilot Randomized Clinical Trial. *JAMA Intern Med,*

*179(10),*1406-1414. Retrieved from: https://pubmed.ncbi. nlm.nih.gov/31380892/

7. Schneider, S. Kingsolver, K., Rosdahl, J. (2014). Physician Coaching to Enhance Well-being: A Qualitative Analysis of a Pilot Intervention. *Science Direct, 10 (6),* 372-379. Retrieved from: https://www.sciencedirect.com/science/article/abs/pii/ S1550830714001542?via%3Dihub

8. Gazelle, G. Liebschutz, J. M., Riess H. (2015). Physician Burnout: Coaching a Way Out. *Journal of General Internal Medicine, 30(4),* 508-513. Retrieved from: https://www.ncbi. nlm.nih.gov/pmc/articles/PMC4371007/

9. Berg, S. (2017, September 11). Family doctors spend 86 minutes of "pajama time" with EHRs nightly. Retrieved from: https://www.ama-assn.org/practice-management/digital/ family-doctors-spend-86-minutes-pajama-time-ehrs-night- ly#:~:text=

10. Cantlupe, J. (2017, November 7). Expert Forum: The rise (and rise) of the healthcare administrator. Retrieved from: https:// www.athenahealth.com/knowledge-hub/practice-manage- ment/expert-forum-rise-and-rise-healthcare-administrator

11. Adriono, L. (2019, November 27). Study reveals surge in US medical malpractice claims costs. Retrieved from: https:// www.insurancebusinessmag.com/us/news/healthcare/ study-reveals-surge-in-us-medical-malpractice-claims- costs-193271.aspx

12. Hill Jr., R. G. Sears, L.M., Melanson, S.W. (November). 4000 Clicks: A Productivity Analysis of Electronic Medical Records in a Community Hospital ED. *American Journal of*

Emergency Medicine, 31(11), 1591-4. Retrieved from: https://pubmed.ncbi.nlm.nih.gov/24060331/

13. Schulte, F., Fry, E. (2019, March 18). Death By 1,000 Clicks: Where Electronic Health Records Went Wrong. Retrieved from: https://khn.org/news/death-by-a-thousand-clicks/

14. Camilleri, M. Gorman, H. (2007). Intestinal Permeability and Irritable Bowel Syndrome. *Neurogastroenterol Motil., 19(7),* 545-52. Retrieved from: https://pubmed.ncbi.nlm.nih.gov/17593135/

15. Smyth, M. C. (2017). Intestinal permeability and autoimmune diseases. Bioscience Horizons: *The International Journal of Student Research, 10(2017).* Retrieved from: https://academic.oup.com/biohorizons/article/doi/10.1093/biohorizons/hzx015/4670557

16. Sharma, S., Awasthi, A., & Singh, S. (2019). Altered Gut Microbiota and Intestinal Permeability in Parkinson's Disease: Pathological Highlight to Management. *Neurosci Lett.* Retrieved from: https://pubmed.ncbi.nlm.nih.gov/31560998/

17. Forkosh, E., & Ilan, Y. (2019). The heart-gut axis: new target for atherosclerosis and congestive heart failure therapy. *Open heart, 6(1),* e000993. Retrieved from: https://www.ncbi.nlm.nih.gov/pmc/articles/PMC6519415/

18. Vighi, G., Marcucci, F., Sensi, L., Di Cara, G., Frati, F. (2008). Allergy and the gastrointestinal system. *Clinical & Experimental Immunology 153 (Suppl 1),* 3–6. Retrieved from: https://www.ncbi.nlm.nih.gov/pmc/articles/PMC2515351/

19. Hadhazy, A. (2010, February 12). Think Twice: How the Gut's "Second Brain" Influences Mood and Well-Being.

Retrieved from: https://www.scientificamerican.com/article/gut-second-brain/

20. Nighot, M. P., Mccarthy, D. M., Ma, T. Y., (2017). Proton Pump Inhibitors (PPI) Induces Increase in Gastric Epithelial Tight Junction Permeability Via Activation of Myosin Light-Chain Kinase. *American Gastroenterological Association,152 (5)*. Retrieved from: https://www.gastrojournal.org/article/S0016-5085(17)33035-4/abstract#articleInformation

21. Nourrisson, C., Wawrzyniak, I., Cian, A., Livrelli, V. (2016). On Blastocystis secreted cysteine proteases: a legumain-activated cathepsin B increases paracellular permeability of intestinal Caco-2 cell monolayers. *Parasitology, 143 (13)*, 1713-1722. Retrieved from: https://www.cambridge.org/core/journals/parasitology/article/on-blastocystis-secreted-cysteine-proteases-a-legumainacti-vated-cathepsin-b-increases-paracellular-permeability-of-in-testinal-caco2-cell-monolayers/77F99318E71293C2466EA-B6A635E472F

22. Fasano, A. (2020, January 31). All disease begins in the (leaky) gut: role of zonulin-mediated gut permeability in the pathogenesis of some chronic inflammatory diseases. Retrieved from: https://www.ncbi.nlm.nih.gov/pmc/articles/PMC6996528/

23. Leech, B., Schloss, J., Steel, A. (2019) Association between increased intestinal permeability and disease: A systematic review. *Advances in Integrative Medicine, 6(1)*, 23-34. Retrieved from: https://www.sciencedirect.com/science/article/abs/pii/S221295881730160X

24. Kazuhide, T., Kubota, Y., Ohira, T., Shimizu, Y., Yamagishi, K., Umesawa, M., Sankai, T., Imano, H., Okada, T.,

Kiyama, M., & Iso, H. (2019) Anger Expression and the Risk of Cardiovascular Disease Among Urban and Rural Japanese Residents: The Circulatory Risk in Communities Study. *Biobehavioral Medicine, 82(2)*, 215-223. Retrieved from: https://journals.lww.com/psychosomaticmedicine/Abstract/2020/02000/Anger_Expression_and_the_Risk_of_Cardiovascular.12.aspx

25. Boggio, P.S., Giglio, A. C. C. K., Nakao C. K., Wingenbach T. S. H., Marques L. M., Koller, S., & Gruber J. (2019) Writing about gratitude increases emotion-regulation efficacy. *The Journal of Positive Psychology*. Retrieved from: https://www.tandfonline.com/doi/full/10.1080/17439760.2019.1651893?scroll=top&needAccess=true

26. Crane, P.K, Walker, R., Hubbard, R. A., Li, Ge, Nathan, D. M., Zheng, H., Haneuse, S., Craft, S., Montine T. J., Khan, S. E., McCormick, W., McCurry, S. M., Bowen, J. D., & Larson, E. B. (2013). Glucose Levels and Risk of Dementia. *New England Journal of Medicine, 369(6)*, 540-8. Retrieved from: https://pubmed.ncbi.nlm.nih.gov/23924004/

27. Pizzorno, J. (2014) Mitochondria—Fundamental to Life and Health. *Integrative Medicine, 13(2)*, 8-15. Retrieved from: https://www.ncbi.nlm.nih.gov/pmc/articles/PMC4684129/

28. Naviaux, R. (2014) Metabolic Features of the Cell Danger Response. *Mitochondrion*, 7-17. Retrieved from: https://pubmed.ncbi.nlm.nih.gov/23981537/

29. Lasalvia, M., Scrima, R., Perna, G., Piccoli, C., Capitanio, N., Biagi, P. F., Schiavulli, L., Ligonzo, T., Centra, M, Casamassima, G., Ermini, A., & Capozzi, V. (2018). Exposure to 1.8 GHz Electromagnetic Fields Affects Morphology, DNA-related Raman Spectra and Mitochondrial Functions

in Human Lympho-Monocytes. *PLoS One, 13(2).* Retrieved from: https://pubmed.ncbi.nlm.nih.gov/29462174/

30. Pereira, A. G., Jaramillo, M. L., Remorse, A. P., Latini, A., Davico, C. E., da Silva, M. L., Muller, Y. M. R., Ammar, D., & Nazari, E. M. (2018) Low-concentration Exposure to Glyphosate-Based Herbicide Modulates the Complexes of the Mitochondrial Respiratory Chain and Induces Mito-chondrial Hyperpolarization in the Danio Rerio Brain. *Chemoshpere, 209,* 353-362. Retrieved from: https://pubmed. ncbi.nlm.nih.gov/29935464/

31. Belyaeva, E. A., Sokolova, T. V., Emelyanova, L. V., & Zakharova, I. O. (2012). Mitochondrial Electron Transport Chain in Heavy Metal-Induced Neurotoxicity: Effects of Cadmium, Mercury, and Copper. *Scientific World Journal.* Retrieved from: https://www.ncbi.nlm.nih.gov/pmc/articles/ PMC3349094/

32. Brewer, J. H., Thrasher, J. D., Straus, D. C., Madison, R. A., & Hooper, D. (2013). Detection of mycotoxins in patients with chronic fatigue syndrome. *Toxins,* 5(4), 605–617. Retrieved from: https://www.ncbi.nlm.nih.gov/pmc/articles/ PMC3705282/

33. Czarny, P., Wigner, P., Piotr, G., & Sliwinski, T. (2018) The interplay between inflammation, oxidative stress, DNA damage, DNA repair and mitochondrial dysfunction in depression. *Progress in Neuro-Psychopharmacology and Bio-logical Psychiatry, 80(C),* 309-321.

34. Eske, J. (2019, April 3). How does oxidative stress affect the body? Retrieved from: https://www.medicalnewstoday.com/ articles/324863

35. Gosh, N., Das, A., Chaffee, S., Roy, S. &Sen, C. K. (2018). Chapter 4 - Reactive Oxygen Species, Oxidative Damage and Cell Death. *Immunity and Inflammation in Health and Disease*, 45-55. Retrieved from: https://www.sciencedirect.com/science/article/pii/B9780128054178000044

36. Harris, D. J., Vine, S. J., Wilson, M. R. (2017). Chapter 12 - Neurocognitive mechanisms of the flow state. *Progress in Brain Research, 234,* 221-243. Retrieved from: https://www.sciencedirect.com/science/article/pii/S0079612317300742

37. McClave, S. A., Snider H. L. (2001) Dissecting the energy needs of the body. *Curr Opin Clin Nutr Metab Care, 4(2),*143-147. Retrieved from: https://pubmed.ncbi.nlm.nih.gov/11224660/

38. Schmidt C. W. (2010). Unraveling Environmental Effects on Mitochondria. Environmental Health Perspectives, *118(7),* A292–A297. Retrieved from: https://www.ncbi.nlm.nih.gov/pmc/articles/PMC2920932/

39. Naviaux, R. K. (2019). Metabolic features and regulation of the healing cycle—A new model for chronic disease pathogenesis and treatment. *Mitochondrion, 46,* 278-297. Retrieved from: https://www.sciencedirect.com/science/article/pii/S1567724918301053?fbclid=IwAR2Sw1Cwi4IPdP6CWikTBpUnZ-qDbMdv3rXRgenoif-y_CVdgS6lZDU_Leg

40. Terman, A., Kurz, T., Navratil, M., Arriaga, E. A., & Brunk, U. T. (2010). Mitochondrial turnover and aging of long-lived postmitotic cells: the mitochondrial-lysosomal axis theory of aging. *Antioxidants & redox signaling, 12(4),* 503–535. Retrieved from: https://www.ncbi.nlm.nih.gov/pmc/articles/PMC2861545/

41. Nicholls, D.G. (2002) Mitochondrial function and dysfunction in the cell: its relevance to aging and aging-related disease. *Int J Biochem Cell Biol., 34(11)*, 1372-1381. Retrieved from: https://pubmed.ncbi.nlm.nih.gov/12200032/

42. Finkel, T. (2011). Telomeres and mitochondrial function. *Circulation Research, 108(8)*, 903–904. Retrieved from: https://www.ncbi.nlm.nih.gov/pmc/articles/PMC3747515/

43. Huskisson, E., Maggini, S., & Ruf, M. (2007). The role of vitamins and minerals in energy metabolism and well-being. *J Int Med Res., 35(3)*, 277-89. Retrieved from:https://www.integrativepro.com/Resources/Integrative-Blog/2015/Back-to-Basics-Mitochondria

44. Dean, W. (2013, September 21). Mitochondrial Dysfunction, Nutrition and Aging. Retrieved from: https://nutritionreview.org/2013/09/mitochondrial-dysfunction/

45. Su, B., Ji YS., Sun, XL., Liu, XH., & Chen, ZY. (2014). Brain-derived neurotrophic factor (BDNF)-induced mitochondrial motility arrest and presynaptic docking contribute to BDNF-enhanced synaptic transmission. *Journal of Biological Chemistry, 289(3)*,1213-1226. Retrieved from: https://pubmed.ncbi.nlm.nih.gov/24302729/

46. Allen, J., Romay-Tallon, R., Brymer, KJ., Caruncho, HJ., & Kalynchuk, LE. (2018). Mitochondria and Mood: Mitochondrial Dysfunction as a Key Player in the Manifestation of Depression. *Front Neuroscience,12(386)*. Retrieved from: https://pubmed.ncbi.nlm.nih.gov/29928190/

47. Sangiovanni, E., Paola, B., Dell'Agli, M, & Calabrese F. (2017). Botanicals as Modulators of Neuroplasticity: Focus

on BDNF. *Neural Plasticity, 22.* Retrieved from: https://www.hindawi.com/journals/np/2017/5965371/#abstract

48. Bailey, D. C., Todt, C.E., Burchfield, S.L., Pressley, A. S., Denney R. D., Snapp I. B., Negga, R., Traynor, W. L., & Fitsanakis, V. A. (2018). Chronic exposure to a glyphosate-containing pesticide leads to mitochondrial dysfunction and increased reactive oxygen species production in Caenorhabditis elegans. *Environ Toxicol Pharmacol. 2018(57),* 46-52. Retrieved from: https://pubmed.ncbi.nlm.nih.gov/29190595/

49. Bailey, D. C., Todt, C.E., Burchfield, S.L., Pressley, A. S., Denney R. D., Snapp I. B., Negga, R., Traynor, W. L., & Fitsanakis, V. A. (2018). Chronic exposure to a glyphosate-containing pesticide leads to mitochondrial dysfunction and increased reactive oxygen species production in Caenorhabditis elegans. *Environ Toxicol Pharmacol. 2018(57),* 46-52. Retrieved from: https://pubmed.ncbi.nlm.nih.gov/29190595/

50. Choi, E.M., Suh, K.S., Rhee, S.Y., Oh, S., Woo, JT., Kim, S. W., Kim, Y.S. Pak, Y. K., Chon, S. (2017). Perfluorooctanoic acid induces mitochondrial dysfunction in MC3T3-E1 osteoblast cells. *J Environ Sci Health A Tox Hazard Subst Environ Eng., 52(3),* 281-289. Retrieved from: https://pubmed.ncbi.nlm.nih.gov/27901621/

51. Rosado-Berrios, C. A., Vélez, C., & Zayas, B. (2011). Mitochondrial permeability and toxicity of diethylhexyl and monoethylhexyl phthalates on TK6 human lymphoblasts cells. *Toxicology in vitro : an international journal published in association with BIBRA, 25(8),* 2010–2016. Retrieved from: https://www.ncbi.nlm.nih.gov/pmc/articles/PMC3217166/

52. Lettieri-Barbato, D., Cannata, S. M., Casagrande, V., Ciriolo, M. R., & Aquilano, K. (2018). Time-controlled fasting prevents aging-like mitochondrial changes induced by persistent dietary fat overload in skeletal muscle. *PloS one, 13(5)*, e0195912. Retrieved from: https://www.ncbi.nlm.nih.gov/pmc/articles/PMC5942780/

53. Sastre, J., Pallardo, F. V., Asuncion J. G, & Vina, J. (2009). Mitochondria, oxidative stress and aging. *Free Radical Research, 32(3)*, 189-198. Retrieved from: https://www.tandfonline.com/doi/abs/10.1080/10715760000300201

54. Mattson, M. P., Longo, V. D., & Harvie, M. (2017). Impact of intermittent fasting on health and disease processes. *Ageing Research Reviews, 39, 46-58.* Retrieved from: *https://www.sciencedirect.com/science/article/pii/S1568163716302513*

55. Mattson, M. P., Moehl, K., Ghena, N., Schmaedick, M., & Cheng, A. (2018). Intermittent metabolic switching, neuroplasticity and brain health. *Nature reviews. Neuroscience, 19(2), 63–80.* Retrieved from: https://www.ncbi.nlm.nih.gov/pmc/articles/PMC5913738/#R66

56. Aly S. M. (2014). Role of intermittent fasting on improving health and reducing diseases. *International journal of health sciences, 8(3)*, V–VI. Retrieved from: https://www.ncbi.nlm.nih.gov/pmc/articles/PMC4257368/

57. Fan, Y., Tang, Y., & Posner, M. (2013). Cortisol Level Modulated by Integrative Meditation in a Dose-dependent Fashion. *Stress & Health, 3(1)*, 65-70. Retrieved from: https://onlinelibrary.wiley.com/doi/abs/10.1002/smi.2497

58. Cooper, B.B. (2013, August 21). What is Meditation and How It Affects Our Brains. Retrieved from: https://buffer.com/resources/how-meditation-affects-your-brain/

59. Ding, X., Tang, Y., Tang R., Posner, M. I. (2014). Improving creativity performance by short-term meditation. *Behav Brain Funct., 10(9)*. Retrieved from: https://behavioralandbrainfunctions.biomedcentral.com/articles/10.1186/1744-9081-10-9#citeas

60. MacLean, K. A., Ferrer, E., Aichele, S. R., Bridwell, D. A., Zanesco, A. P., Jacobs, T. L., King, B. G., Rosenberg, E. L., Sahdra, B. K., Shaver, P. R., Wallace, B. A., Mangun, G. R., & Saron, C. D. (2010). Intensive meditation training improves perceptual discrimination and sustained attention. *Psychological science, 21(6)*, 829–839. Retrieved from: https://www.ncbi.nlm.nih.gov/pmc/articles/PMC3132583/

61. Mrazek, M. D., Franklin, M. S., Phillips, D. T., Baird, B., & Schooler, J. W. (2013). Mindfulness Training Improves Working Memory Capacity and GRE Performance While Reducing Mind Wandering. *Psychological Science, 24(5)*, 776–781. Retrieved from: https://journals.sagepub.com/doi/abs/10.1177/0956797612459659?rss=1&;ssource=m-fr&#articleCitationDownloadContainer

62. 6 Ways Meditation Increases Your Intelligence & Raises Your IQ. (n.d.) Retrieved from: https://eocinstitute.org/meditation/increase-your-intelligence-with-meditation/

63. Black DS, O'Reilly GA, Olmstead R, Breen EC, Irwin MR. (2015). Mindfulness Meditation and Improvement in Sleep Quality and Daytime Impairment Among Older

Adults With Sleep Disturbances: A Randomized Clinical Trial. *JAMA Intern Med., 175(4),* 494–501. Retrieved from: https://jamanetwork.com/journals/jamainternalmedicine/fullarticle/2110998

64. Semalty, M., Adhikari, L., Semwal, D., Chauhan, A., Akash M., Rupali, K., & Semalty, A. (2017) A Comprehensive Review on Phytochemistry and Pharmacological Effects of Stinging Nettle (Urtica dioica). *Current Traditional Medicine, 3(3),* 156-167. Retrieved from: https://www.ingentaconnect.com/content/ben/ctm/2017/00000003/00000003/art00003

65. Salve, J., Pate, S., Debnath, K., Langade, D. (2019) Adaptogenic and Anxiolytic Effects of Ashwagandha Root Extract in Healthy Adults: A Double-blind, Randomized, Placebo-controlled Clinical Study. *Cureus,* 11(12): e6466. Retrieved from: https://www.cureus.com/articles/25730-adaptogenic-and-anxiolytic-effects-of-ashwagandha-root-extract-in-healthy-adults-a-double-blind-randomized-placebo-controlled-clinical-study

66. Medical Symptom/Toxicity Questionnaire. Retrieved from: https://drhyman.com/downloads/MSQ_Fillable.pdf

67. Fujioka, N., Ransom, B. W., Carmella, S. G., Upadhyaya, P., Lindgren,B. R., Roper-Batker, A., Hatsukami, D. K., Fritz, V. A., Rohwer, C., & Hecht, S. S. (2016). Harnessing the Power of Cruciferous Vegetables: Developing a Biomarker for Brassica Vegetable Consumption Using Urinary 3,3☒-Diindolylmethane. *Cancer Prev Res, 9(10),* 788-793. Retrieved from: https://cancerpreventionresearch.aacrjournals.org/content/9/10/788.abstract

68. Thomson, C.A., Chow, HH. S., Wertheim B.C., Roe, D. J., Stopeck, A., Maskarinec, G., Altbach, M., Chalasani,

P., Huang, C., Strom, M. B., Galons, J-P., Thompson, P.A. (2017). A randomized, placebo-controlled trial of diindolyl-methane for breast cancer biomarker modulation in patients taking tamoxifen. *Breast Cancer Res Treat.,165(1),* 97-107. Retrieved from: https://pubmed.ncbi.nlm.nih.gov/28560655/

69. Lu, J. G., Akinola, M., & Mason, M. F. (2017). "Switching On" creativity: Task switching can increase creativity by reducing cognitive fixation. *Organizational Behavior and Human Decision Processes,139,* 63-75. Retrieved from: https://www.sciencedirect.com/science/article/abs/pii/S074959781630108X

70. Kotler, S. (2014, February 25). Flow States and Creativity: Can you train people to be more creative? Retrieved from: https://www.psychologytoday.com/us/blog/the-playing-field/201402/flow-states-and-creativity

71. Conner, T. S., DeYoung C. G., & Silvia P. J. (2018) Everyday creative activity as a path to flourishing. *The Journal of Positive Psychology, 13(2),* 181-189. Retrieved from: https://www.tandfonline.com/doi/abs/10.1080/17439760.2016.1257049

72. Flock, E. (2019 November, 5). Burnout is rampant among doctors and nurses. Can the arts help? Retrieved from: https://www.pbs.org/newshour/arts/burnout-is-rampant-among-doctors-and-nurses-can-the-arts-help

73. Friedman, S. E., Levy, E. I. MD, Owen, M., Vossler, A. H., Friedman, E. P., Hussain, S. (2018). Commentary: Flow State (Trading the Sweat Spot for the Sweet Spot): A Roadmap to Measure and Enhance Workplace Growth and Well-Being. *Neurosurgery, 83(6),* E262–E265. Retrieved from: https://academic.oup.com/neurosurgery/article-abstract/83/6/E262/5099456?redirectedFrom=fulltext

74. Cooper, B.B. (2013, July 25). How Naps Affect Your Brain and Why You Should Have One Every Day. Retrieved from: https://buffer.com/resources/how-naps-affect-your-brain-and-why-you-should-have-one-every-day/

75. Currey, M (2013). Daily Rituals: How Artists Work. New York: Alfred A. Knopf.

76. Gregoire, C. (2013, July 17). The One Thing These Crazy Successful People Do Every Morning. Retrieved from: https://www.huffpost.com/entry/the-first-thing-these-suc_n_3588482

77. Roger Bannister (2020, June 14). In *Wikipedia*. Retrieved from: https://en.wikipedia.org/wiki/Roger_Bannister

78. Runner Demographics- Statistics and Research (2017, March 23). Retrieved from: https://www.5kevents.org/demographics.html

79. Anderson, P. (2018, May 8). Doctors' Suicide Rate Highest of Any Profession. Retrieved from: https://www.webmd.com/mental-health/news/20180508/doctors-suicide-rate-highest-of-any-profession#1

80. Jackson Healthcare. (2013, June 11). Forty-two Percent of Physicians Unhappy with Job. Retrieved from: https://www.prnewswire.com/news-releases/forty-two-percent-of-physicians-unhappy-with-job-211032521.html

81. New Findings Confirm Predictions on Physician Shortage. (2019, April 23). Retrieved from: https://www.aamc.org/news-insights/press-releases/new-findings-confirm-predictions-physician-shortage

82. Why are SMA's Beneficial? Retrieved from: https:// my.clevelandclinic.org/patients/information/shared-medical-appointments/why-are-smas-beneficial

83. Richard, A., Rohrmann, S., Vandeleur, C.L., Schmid, M., Barth, J., Eichholzer, M. (2017) Loneliness is adversely associated with physical and mental health and lifestyle factors: Results from a Swiss national survey. *PLoS One,12(7)*. Retrieved from: https://pubmed.ncbi.nlm.nih.gov/28715478/

84. Goldstein, M. R., Lewis, G. F., Newman, R., Brown, J. M., Bobashev, G., Kilpatrick, L., Seppälä, E. M., Fishbein, D. H., & Meleth, S. (2016). Improvements in well-being and vagal tone following a yogic breathing-based life skills workshop in young adults: Two open-trial pilot studies. *International journal of yoga, 9(1)*, 20–26. Retrieved from: https://www.ncbi.nlm.nih.gov/pmc/articles/PMC4728954/

85. Sullivan, J., Thorn, N., Amin, M., Mason, K., Lue, N., & Nawzir, M. (2019) Using simple acupressure and breathing techniques to improve mood, sleep and pain management in refugees: a peer-to-peer approach in a Rohingya refugee camp. *Intervention, 17*, 252-8. Retrieved from: http://www.interventionjournal.org/article.asp?issn=1571-8883;year=2019;volume=17;issue=2;spage=252;epage=258;aulast=Sullivan

86. Right Brain Rescue. https://rightbrainrescue.com/

87. Baker, D. W. (2017, May 5). The Joint Commission's Pain Standards: Origins and Evolution. Retrieved from: https://www.jointcommission.org/-/media/tjc/documents/resources/pain-management/pain_std_history_web_version_05122017pdf.pdf?db=web&hash=E7D12A5C3BE9DF031F3D-8FE0D8509580

88. Strang, C. (n.d.) Department of Psychology College of Arts and Sciences. Retrieved from: https://www.uab.edu/cas/psychology/people/faculty/christianne-strang

89. American Art Therapy Association. https://arttherapy.org/

90. Right Brain Rescue. https://rightbrainrescue.com/

ACKNOWLEDGEMENTS

Thank you to my favorite soulmate, CJ. My soul knew you long before my heart realized it. You are the master of lines...because you know how to overstep them so predictably, leaving everyone in stitches. Thank you for living life with me, as imperfectly perfect, messy, and real as it is. I couldn't imagine another person I'd want to pick up my earplugs scattered around the house.

To my sparkly children, each of you with a spectacular personality and fire of your own. Thank you for everything you are and everything you will become. I have the easiest job in the world as your mother: I just have to get out of your way. You are all incredible humans. No written book could possibly contain all the love I have for you.

Thank you to the small but potent league of kindred spirits that show up for me in their fullest and inspire me at all times: Katie, Tony, Jill, Lisa, Petra. Thank you for listening to hours of my word vomit, for sharing the same snarky humor, for geeking out about the same things, for embracing my imperfections, and for cheering me on during some of the darkest times.

Thank you to my OG squad from KCOM medical school: The Group. For over twenty-four years, we've laughed and cried through weddings and divorces, road trips and final exams, births and deaths. Nowhere in the world is unspoken conversation easier and more profoundly stimulating than with people who inherently "get it."

Thank you to my mom and dad, who instilled a gritty stubbornness that has led me to all things wondrous. You encouraged me to ask "why" and never stop exploring with my imagination. Thank you for doing your absolute best to give us opportunities that enriched our right brains.

Thank you to Amy for being the most brilliant virtual-turned-real assistant any micropractice doc could ask for. You collaborate with a perfect balance of diligent work and sassy fun. You think ten steps ahead of me. I owe all things savage to you.

Thank you to Patrick Bodell and his phenomenal team at Synqronus Communications for your talent at web design, and your creativity and input in the early stages of *Right Brain Rescue.* Without your guidance, this little "baby" wouldn't have been delivered into the world, despite being dilated to nine centimeters for what seemed like forever.

Thank you to all of those not specifically mentioned who are an equally important part of my story, but didn't make the paragraphs in this book. There are innumerable stories left untold, and I'm grateful for your stardust in this magical world.

Thank you to all the mentors, business associates, and programs that are a significant part of my colorful tapestry:

- A.T. Still University Class of 2000 (previously Kirksville College of Osteopathic Medicine)

- Metropolitan Hospital Family Medicine Residency (Grand Rapids, Michigan)

- St. John's Clinic in St. Robert, Missouri

- Brodhead Clinic as part of Monroe Clinic, Wisconsin

- Dr. Jeffrey Bland of the Institute of Functional Medicine at www.ifm.org

- Dr. Deborah Lathrop as my confidant and for her work on physician burnout

- Dr. Heather Fork for her assistance in coaching physicians at www.DoctorsCrossing.com

- James Maskell and his stellar posse at *Evolution of Medicine's Practice Accelerator* (www.GoEvoMed.com)

- Dr. Errin Weisman, DO at www.truthrxs.com for her badass work on burnout in women physicians

- Barry Callen for his creativity and ingenuity in shaping my interactive workshops

- The Monroe Chamber of Commerce in Monroe, Wisconsin for helping our small businesses thrive

- Jason Teteak and *Rule the Room* to polish my public speaking skills at www.ruletheroompublicspeaking.com

- Elizabeth Gilbert, Brene Brown, Scott Barry Kaufman, and Steven Kotler, my personal heroes and transformationally creative muses

- *Self-Publishing School* staff at www.selfpublishingschool. com, specifically Gary Williams, who is the most chipper cheerleader and book coach

- Qat Wanders and her eagle-eyed team at Wandering Words Media at www.wanderingwordsmedia.com for editing the hell out of this baby

THANK YOU FOR
READING MY BOOK!

Come play with your Right Brain in my
Free 10-Day Creative AF Challenge
www.rightbrainrescue.com

I eat feedback for breakfast, so please GIMME SOME!
Please, leave me an honest review on Amazon
to let me know what you thought of the book.

COLOR IT *FORWARD*:
This makes the perfect gift for your medical school graduate
or favorite physician during the next Doctor's Day celebration.
Keep coloring outside the lines!

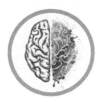

ABOUT THE AUTHOR

Lara Salyer, DO, IFMCP, is an award-winning, small-town family physician who "colors outside the lines of a typical doctor." She strategically resigned from her employed position in 2016 to open a holistic private practice in functional medicine. She believes "a patient's health is directly proportional to their physician's teaching ability." She also believes most woes can be cured with a great hair day and matte lipstick.

Driven by a passion to impart sustainable integrative health to the masses, she leverages technology to build a cohesive tribe of wellness in her community by hosting innovative group medical visits, online health education, as well as traditional individual services. She uses her experience and obsessively organized collection of notes to assist other health professionals in building their own creative micropractice through professional mentorship.

When she's not working, Lara writes, draws, and speaks about the intersection of creative flow state and medicine. She loves any excuse to skip an afternoon of Muber duty and give a keynote on stage. Take a photo. It's the only time she will wear high heels. Otherwise, she prefers running shoes.

She is the founder of the online "creativity incubator" program,

Right Brain Rescue, and the illustrator of the book written by her son, *The Colorful Teeth* by Beckett D. Smith. She lives in Monroe, Wisconsin, with her favorite physician husband of twenty-plus Earth years, their three magnificently unique children, a manic dog, and infinite piles of laundry.

WORK WITH ME

TAKE THE FREE "10-DAY CREATIVE AF" CHALLENGE!
Sign up at www.rightbrainrescue.com

TO IGNITE YOUR CREATIVE MUSE:
Right Brain Rescue is the first complete at-home program that intertwines groundbreaking neuroscience with interactive activities, downloadable workbooks, practical tips to build sustainable habits, engaging videos, delightful creative exercises, and delicious recipes. Try a small sample or enroll in the Right Brain Rescue Complete Course at www.rightbrainrescue.com. Use code **BOOK50** to save $50.

FOR PROSPECTIVE PATIENTS INTERESTED IN FUNCTIONAL MEDICINE CARE:
You must be willing to travel to Monroe, Wisconsin. Access my online educational classes and read about my services on www.drlarasalyer.com. Schedule a phone Strategy Session to chat about your medical case and see if we're a good fit to work together ("Services > Individual > Become a Patient")

FOR HEALTH PROFESSIONALS:
I offer individualized mentorship services for those looking to build a creative medical micropractice. Head to www.rightbrainrescue.

com for all the goodies like a free Micropractice Masterclass (learn my top tips on becoming a colorful healthcare entrepreneur) or downloadable Medical Infographics (with editable templates to customize for your own office). You can read more about me on my website www.drlarasalyer.com and book a complimentary Discovery Call to see if personalized mentorship is the spark you need ("Services > Individual > For Medical Professionals").

FOR EVENT PLANNERS AND HOSPITAL ADMINISTRATORS:

I love dealing drugs from center stage. Creative flow state is the most entertaining way to inspire a crowd to think differently about their physiology, stress and daily play. If you are looking to freshen up your next event, let's talk about my keynote services and interactive workshops on a Discovery Call. You can apply for this at www.drlarasalyer.com (under "Services > Public > Speaking Services").